"You don't have to be a miserable, lonely, pregnant lesbian to adore Andrea Askowitz's awfully funny story. Anyone who enjoys schadenfreude, laugh-out-loud asides, and frank depictions of biological horrors will love this wonderful book. You will read it dog-eared and quote the most outrageous parts at length to all your friends."

—Jennifer Traig, author of *Devil in the Details: Scenes from an Obsessive Girlhood*

"Andrea Askowitz hits on all the key points of surviving pregnancy as a single lesbian—dealing with donor choices and unreliable exes, coping with hormonal hell and morning sickness, and figuring out exactly what one will need for life with a new baby (and no, a new tent isn't the best baby registry item!). Mandatory reading for all lesbian mothers-to-be."

—Rachel Pepper, author of *The Ultimate Guide to Pregnancy for Lesbians*

"Funny, sad, unblinkingly honest—I would give this one to any pregnant friend and a few who aren't."

—Joyce Maynard, author of *At Home in the World*, *The Usual Rules*, and *To Die For*

Andrea Askowitz is "warm, funny and filthy."

—Slate.com

"Andrea is the lesbian Anne Lamott. Her book makes me want to donate sperm."

—Taylor Negron, actor

# my miserable, lonely, lesbian pregnancy

by andrea askowitz

CLEIS
PRESS

Cleis Press Inc., P.O. Box 14697, San Francisco, California 94114
Printed in the United States.
Cover design: Scott Idleman
Cover photograph: Gary S. Chapman/Getty Images
Author photograph: Stephanie Howard
Text design: Frank Wiedemann
Cleis logo art: Juana Alicia
First Edition.
10 9 8 7 6 5 4 3 2 1

Author's note: Fees and information mentioned in the book are based on
2003 California Cryobank pricing and policies.

Some names and numbers have been changed.

Library of Congress Cataloging-in-Publication Data

Askowitz, Andrea.
  My miserable, lonely, lesbian pregnancy / by Andrea Askowitz.
      p. cm.
  ISBN 978-1-57344-315-9 (pbk. : alk. paper)
  1. Askowitz, Andrea. 2. Lesbian mothers--Biography. 3. Pregnancy. I.
Title.
  HQ75.53.A78 2008
  306.874'3092--dc22
  [B]
                                        2007050324

For Tashi.
You are extraordinary.
I love you more than I ever could have imagined.

*"Be who you are and say what you feel, because those who mind don't matter, and those who matter don't mind."*

—Dr. Seuss

# First Trimester

## CONCEPTION

At 11 A.M. I rush past my office mates and out the door. I have a 12:30 appointment at the Kaiser Infertility Clinic. I say, "See you later, I'm going to get pregnant."

First, I drive to the California Cryobank. I walk down a long, dark hallway to the pickup window and look around for men to try to get a glimpse of the kind of guy who donates here, but the donors seem to use a separate entrance. I consider the possibility of bumping into someone I know, but the hall is empty. There is no waiting room, just a glass window that slides open when I ring the bell.

A woman in a lab coat charges my credit card $320 and hands over my baby's daddy—a vial half the size of my pinkie, encased in a freezing tank inside a three-foot-high box with arrows and the words "This Way Up." I tuck the sperm behind the passenger seat and head to the clinic.

The day is bright and blue and mild. A fine day to get pregnant. I take Sunset, which is tree-lined for miles, and I'm thinking it's one of the prettiest streets in Los Angeles, until I get farther east and then Sunset becomes as ugly as any other strip-mall stretch of LA.

The music this morning is my favorite, classic hits from the '70s and '80s. I haven't moved on. In 2003, I'm still listening to ABBA and Fleetwood Mac. The windows are open, and I'm singing, "Oh Oh, dream weavah, I believe you can get me through the niiiihhiiight."

I carry the sperm box inside—it's unwieldy but not heavy—and hand it over to the nurse for defrosting. This is my second attempt, so I know the routine.

The first time, I brought my best friend Stephanie, a professional photographer who took pictures like she was the proud dad: me walking in with the loot, me in the waiting room eating a peach Danish, me on the table with my feet in the stirrups, and even some crotch shots of the sperm going in.

I'm lucky: most people don't get good photos of conception.

The last time, Kate wanted to come, but we agreed it would be too hard. We ate Thai food the night before, and she cried over the tom ka gai, our favorite soup—chicken with coconut milk, medium spicy. Damn her for not getting her shit together in time to be my co-mom. Kate is so pretty and gentle, and I dreamed of her holding our baby. And holding me. I waited six years for her to grow up.

We broke up several months ago. A divorce, really. We weren't legally married, but we were family. We shared a health insurance policy.

Another woman's in the clinic waiting room, apparently alone, but wearing a wedding band, and a man and a woman are sitting together. We smile and nod at each other. I wonder if we're all waiting for our sperm to defrost.

Although I'm by myself this time, I don't feel lonely. I feel cool and confident, like I'm doing my part. The war in Iraq started a few weeks ago, and I have been feeling powerless. I want to be more effective in creating peace in the world, and this war seems beyond my control, no matter how many peace rallies I go to. But today, as I sit looking up at the Matisse print, the one of the big-hipped woman dancing with no feet, I think: Maybe this is my contribution. No pressure on the kid, but maybe the kid will be a peacemaker—a sort of modern-day Jesus Christ, as this Jew understands Jesus—someone who can speak the language of those in power and at the same time befriend those who are disempowered. And if this doesn't resemble the Immaculate Conception, I don't know what does.

### WEEK 1, DAY 5
I'm on our annual family vacation in Key West, Florida, with my mom and her boyfriend, Bob, my brother, Tony, sister-in-law, Lisa, and my three nieces.

My family knows I've been inseminated; that the sperm I bought at the sperm bank has been squirted into my uterus by a very capable nurse, and we are waiting for the two-week mark so I can take the pregnancy test. The whole time, I make excuses for not carrying my suitcase or the groceries: "I can't, on account of the twins."

I'm hoping for twins. My mom says I'm crazy, but I insist it will be good for the twins. They'll need each other.

### WEEK 1, DAY 7
We've been sitting inside all morning because the planned activities have been rained out. My brother is big on planned, family activities. But today there will be no mini golf or hunting for seashells. Tony is talking on his cell phone, pacing the living room. I'm happy lounging around with my nieces, but

if I have to play another round of animal Charades, I might swim to Cuba.

Danielle, who's 5, comes and sits so close to me on the couch I can feel her breath when she talks. She says, "Andrea, will you play animals, again?"

As soon as she smiles up at me I realize I'd do anything for her. I get off the couch, gather the other girls, and start the game. I put my hands together, lean over, and slowly rock side to side for my best elephant imitation. Danielle guesses elephant, so it's her turn. She stands in front of us, touches her cheek with her chubby finger, as if she's thinking, and then puts her hands together, leans over, and slowly rocks side to side. Rachel, who's 8, rolls her eyes like a teenager and says, "Elephant." We all laugh hard.

Sleep is something I used to do well, but tonight I'm staring into the darkness.

Getting into bed with Kate was my favorite thing in the world. She felt like a heated waterbed. She didn't like it when I said that. "You just love me so you can cuddle up with me in bed," she said.

"Well...that's not the only reason; I also love your boobs," I said. I was flirting.

I'm sharing a room with Rachel and Danielle. The two of them are snoozing in the next bed, so I can't turn on the light to read.

This is the way it is in my family, when you're single. You're not an equal citizen with adult status. My brother, who has a wife and three kids, has a louder voice when it comes to family decisions, so Tony and Lisa get their own room on family vacations. I'm relegated to the children's room.

Tomorrow I'll take a pregnancy test. I'm not looking forward to trying to decipher the stick. I have plenty of experience peeing on sticks, and still, I'm no expert. For five months leading up to insemination, I peed on more than a hundred sticks to determine when I was ovulating. The pregnancy test works the same way.

First, hold the plastic apparatus, the approximate size of a flat highlighter pen, pointing the tip into your stream of urine for seven seconds. Be careful not to splash into the tiny test window or get pee on your hand. Then replace the lid, put the stick on a level, dry surface, and wait five minutes. Two lines should appear in the window. The test line on a positive stick will be darker than the control line, or equally dark.

The test line on my ovulation stick was always slightly lighter than the control line, or so it seemed. I was never sure. The lines were small, like pencil scratches, and their shades of purple or pink or blue were subtle and indistinct. I wanted two equally dark lines so badly I didn't trust myself. I needed a second opinion.

I did two tests a day for ten days for five cycles. At $6 a stick, I spent $600 before spending $225 more on a computerized system, which requires inserting the pee stick into a slot for the computer to read. For all I shelled out, I should own the pee stick company, Clear Plan Easy.

Now that I think about it, I should call the company to tell them their sticks aren't *clear* and they're not *easy,* and they know it, otherwise there'd be no need for a computer. I'll demand a case or two for free. I'll say, "Listen, I'm not like the other girls. I have to time everything exactly right: detect ovulation, buy my sperm, drive it across town, defrost, get inseminated, and hope my sperm meets my egg just as my egg is making its way into the uterus. I can't just lie back and get fucked."

I wake up from a dream at 6 A.M. In the dream, I peed on a pregnancy test stick the size of a poster board. In seconds, two thick hot-pink lines appeared across the poster. I saw a little girl, maybe a 1-year-old, tall for her age, with brown curly hair, wearing white terry-cloth footy pajamas. She looked like a boy, but she was a girl.

I go to the bathroom and pee on a stick. My hand is steady and my stream precise. I place the stick on the windowsill and try to look away, thinking a watched stick never pinks, but I can't keep my eyes off. Two pink lines emerge. The lines are dark and decisive.

I get into bed and lie awake for half an hour. I'm pregnant.

I got pregnant after five years of planning, because, for a lesbian, there are no accidents. It didn't actually take me five years to conceive; I just talked about it and thought about it and took my temperature every morning for a very long time. But right now I'm having a little trouble breathing. Holy shit, what have I done?

I've always wanted to be a mom. My mother tells me that when I was not even 3 years old I'd say things like "When I'm a mommy, I'll make wee-wee in the potty." Motherhood was never a role I questioned.

A lot of people ask me why I want children, and anyone entering parenthood should have to answer this question. But when I asked my straight, married friends why they wanted children, three of them said, "No one ever asked me that. People just ask when."

When I asked Janet, who's been one of my best friends since we were 15, she said she wanted to create life out of the love she shares with her husband. A beautiful reason, but I don't have that option.

I want to have a child because I'm a woman. I feel a biological urge, like a yearning in my heart and gut. Pregnancy and motherhood are experiences I crave. I want to connect myself to generations before and after me. I want to belong to the society of mothers. I want to give love. I want to recognize myself in another person. I want to create.

And I'm almost 35; time is running out.

I've always dreamed of a family of my own. In the dream, I'm making homemade baby food: baking squash and scooping out the soft middle. I bike to the store to get diapers with my baby, who's wearing a tiny helmet in the bike seat on the back. I hold hands with my co-mom as we get teary watching our baby enter kindergarten. I make drums out of oatmeal containers and homemade Play-Doh with plenty of salt, flour, water, and a touch of cream of tartar. I make flash cards to practice the times tables and I coach Little League.

When I came out almost 13 years ago, I didn't think my chance for motherhood was doomed, like my own mother thought. I was doubling my chances. I envisioned two wedding dresses and two pregnant bellies.

Also, as long as I can remember, I've wanted to be pregnant. In my fantasy, I'm spending lazy afternoons in the south of Spain, getting bigger and happier each day. I have no cares. I'm gestating. I wander along the cobblestone streets eating olives and improving my Spanish with the locals. At night, I dance naked in a clearing in the woods, making moon shadows with my belly. When I get into bed with my lover, the white, cool sheets and the softness of her body comfort me.

I do yoga through the ninth month, when *malasana*, the squatting pose, brings on contractions. I announce at the end of yoga class that my baby is coming. Everyone cheers. A few hours later, with my lover by my side, our baby is born.

That was my fantasy. In reality, I broke up with Kate six

months ago. We thought we would create a family together, and right now, I'm having trouble letting go of that dream.

At 7 A.M., my nieces wake up and look over at me from the next bed. When I see their eyes, I sit up. "I'm pregnant," I say.

Rachel, the oldest one, says, "Now you have a real baby in your tummy."

The two of them run into their parents' room and scream the news. I stand in the hallway listening. They bound upstairs and tell my mom and Bob. Everyone cheers like crazy.

## WEEK 2, DAY 2

I call Janet, and she screeches. I can hear her jumping up and down. I say, "Be careful, you have a baby in there."

She says, "I knew it, I knew it. We're four months apart." Janet is four months pregnant with her second.

I call Stephanie, and she says, "Holy shit!"

"I know," I say.

I am calm until I dial Kate's number, which I know so well it seems to dial by itself. My heart starts pounding. I hang up. I go to the bathroom and look at myself in the mirror. I lift my shirt. No sign. I go back to the phone. I pick it up. I put it down. I pick it up and dial.

"Hi, it's Andrea."

"Are you okay?" She sounds alarmed.

"I'm pregnant."

"Oh Angie, I am so happy for you." She gets quiet, and I think she might be crying. Kate is not afraid to cry.

"Thanks," I say.

"How do you feel?"

"Um, a mix. Happy. Scared. Lots of things."

"I hope the kid's like you," she says.

"Like me?" My eyes well up when she says this. After three breakups and years of back and forth, I wonder how

Kate can still like me at all. I don't know what to say.

"Take care of yourself and the baby," she says. "I love you."

My mom sees me making phone calls. She says, "What's the matter with you? You shouldn't tell anyone until after the first trimester."

I know the likelihood of a miscarriage is one in four, or possibly higher, and that there's a Jewish superstition to keep quiet for three months, but I can't keep the news to myself. I also know that if I have a miscarriage, telling my friends won't be the hard part. I'd have to tell Kate. She's the one I want with me when there's an emotional crisis.

I say, "Mom, get out of my business. If I have a miscarriage, I'll talk to my friends about it."

I call Todd, a friend from high school: the most obnoxious kid in class, but funny, so I liked him. He's really more a fan than a friend. On the one hand, Todd loves me so much that I enjoy the attention. On the other hand, his reasons for loving me are absurd and insulting. He has this idea that I was popular in high school and pulls out our high school yearbook at every dinner party he hosts and talks about my high school achievements. He also considers having a lesbian friend a mark of social status.

"Todd, I'm pregnant."

"Wow, congratulations. Mazel tov. Andrea, may the world be blessed with your child."

He has become very religious since high school. "Thank you," I say.

He says, "You're not telling anyone, are you?"

"If I'm telling you, I've already told forty people, but thanks for that advice."

He says, "People will cast an evil eye on you."

"What the hell does that mean?"

"People will be jealous and try to bring bad luck."

"Is that what you're doing?" I say. My ears get hot. "Is this some archaic, Jewish paranoid belief? I don't think like that, and I don't appreciate you even suggesting something so freaky."

"Just be careful."

"You know, fuck you. Good-bye."

This conversation leaves me extremely sad. I want to call Robin, my best friend from high school, to tell her how crazy Todd has gotten. I want to tell her I'm pregnant. But she died just over a year ago from cancer. They found it during the birth of her second child.

The doctors thought Robin had a fibroid tumor, something pretty common during pregnancy. They thought hormones were fueling it out of control.

At 32 weeks, two months too soon, her baby went into distress. They did a C-section and found cancer everywhere. They cut out her appendix, uterus, ovaries, part of her colon, and part of her bladder. Her baby was healthy, but Robin died six months later.

### WEEK 4, DAY 3

Todd has left me three voice messages since we talked. Yesterday he said, "The world is so lucky you are pregnant. We are truly going to have a blessed child."

Today he says: "What did your parents do? I want their secret, because we want a child just like you, Andrea: confident, fun, cute, and curly. Oh, and a fast runner." I was on the track team in high school.

I tell Stephanie, my friend since elementary school, what Todd said. "Yeah, I hope the kid's like you too," she says. Holy shit, Kate said the same thing. What are they talking about? A kid like *me*?

"I'm not so nice," I say. I feel like I might cry. "Todd

thinks we're best friends, but I told him he's forty-first on my list."

"Well, maybe you should try to keep some of your thoughts to yourself," Steph says.

I call Todd. "Thanks for your nice messages. I don't know what's wrong with me. I yelled at my mom's boyfriend for defending the war. I told my mom to get out of my business. I'm pissy and snapping at everybody. And this is so embarrassing, but everything makes me want to cry. And I'm still mad about the evil eye comment."

He says, "Just because you're quick to snap doesn't mean people don't deserve it."

I like Todd again.

## Week 5, day 2

I show Stephanie my thighs. "Look how chubby I am already."

Stephanie has the kind of beauty other girls in high school were intimidated by. As an adult, people always tell me how pretty she is. They tell her too, and she is gracious. She is dark, with a strong nose, a cross between Cher and Meryl Streep. She holds herself tall and serene. And even though she has always been thinner and taller, we wear the same size pants. Since elementary school, we've traded our jeans back and forth—Gloria Vanderbilt, Jordache, Edwin, Levi's, and Diesel. We're not into labels anymore.

A few years ago, Stephanie moved to Los Angeles. Now we live in the same city, the first time since we left home for college. Still, we grew up together. We've always written long letters back and forth and visited often. Lately we talk every day.

We'll have a dinner party at my house, and Steph will help cook and then clean up, and after everyone leaves we'll sit on the couch and talk for hours. At 2 A.M. she'll stand up to go. She'll say, "I better go. Bye."

I'll say, "Oh yeah, bye. I have to buy my mom a birthday present." And we'll talk for another hour about commercialism and family and obligation and what our mothers did to make us the way we are. Then it will be too late to drive home, and she'll stay the night.

She says, "Your thighs are a little chubby. Hey, I'm not going to listen to you complain for nine months."

"Only eight more," I say.

## WEEK 5, DAY 3

I go to an early pregnancy class at Kaiser, my HMO. We are sitting in a big, charmless classroom—six man–woman couples and me. I'm sure they have no idea I'm a lesbian and went to the sperm store to get half my baby's genetics. They probably think I left my husband at home. I decide I hate them for thinking I left my husband at home and now I'm preoccupied with setting them straight. I'll ask a question starting with "As a lesbian..." No. That would sound idiotic. I remind myself of Lois, the one lesbian in college who said, "As a lesbian..." every time she spoke about anything. Lois was at least six feet tall. One day in women's studies class she hiked up her pant leg to show off her rugby bruises. I gasped when I saw her hairy leg—hairier than my dad's. She could probably sense I was a lesbian before I did, which might be why she was compelled to mention how most women come out after college. She looked right at me once when she explained a phenomenon she called pre-lesbian tension, or PLT. PLT is when a woman who is not out exhibits heightened interest in the life—dating patterns, classes, meal schedule—of an out lesbian.

I may have been a little bit interested in Lois's life, but mostly I thought she was a freak. In retrospect, I see that

Lois was brave and cool to announce she was a lesbian; I needed to know other lesbians existed. The people in this room do not need to know a lesbian exists. Or do they, since clearly a lesbian does exist in this room? Maybe they need to know I'm doing this alone. I wonder if they'd feel sorry for me. Fuck this. I shouldn't have to do this alone. Kate should be here writing notes about what spotting looks like. She should keep the date in her calendar for when I need to call for my amniocentesis appointment. But would she? Could she take care of me? Could she take care of me and a baby? Could I take care of her?

Every other ceiling pane is a fluorescent light. The other women don't look pregnant like I do. Or maybe I just look fat.

We're looking at drawings of the fetus inside the womb on crusty posters that look like they've been around since the '70s. This is the most exciting event in my life, and this class is more boring than traffic school.

The teacher tells us that doctors count gestation starting from the first day of the last menstrual period, because most couples don't know the exact day they conceive. Full term is 40 weeks from the first day of the last period.

I know the exact day I conceived, but according to doctors, I am two weeks more pregnant than I thought and, therefore, two weeks closer to the second trimester. Nausea usually subsides in the second trimester, the teacher tells us, so I will accept this news.

The teacher asks us what else we'd like to get out of today's class. Not one of the women raises her hand. One of the men says, "My wife is so moody I don't know what to do."

The teacher spends the next 45 minutes talking about the supporter's role as husband and lover. What he should expect to feel throughout the pregnancy. How his moods will go up and down. How he should handle sex. Ways he should deal with stress. I want to scream: *This is HER turn!* It is not like me to keep quiet, but for some reason I am too nervous to speak.

Finally, we move on to what the pregnant women might experience. We learn that cramps are normal. Major cramps could be a problem. Spotting is normal. Vomiting for 24 hours is a problem.

The woman closest to me is eating Saltines. The sound of her eating makes me want to retch. I wish she would offer me one.

## WEEK 7, DAY 4

Janet sends me a pregnancy book, *Your Pregnancy Week by Week, 4th Edition.* She has a 2–year-old and is pregnant with her second. She is smart. She's a newspaper reporter. I trust she knows which pregnancy book is best.

Each chapter, for a different week, shows a detailed sketch of the fetus. I skip to week 7. The thing looks like a bloated seahorse. The tiny drawing, only as big as the fingernail on my pinkie, is labeled "actual size."

Week 10 shows the fetus the size of a small plum, week 11, a large lime, week 17, an open hand.

I start reading from the beginning. The first chapter lists possible maladies for me: anemia, asthma, urinary tract infection, diabetes, hypertension. The next chapters explain ways the baby could become retarded or crippled or infertile. If I eat mercury-contaminated fish, the child could get cerebral palsy. If I get rubella in the first 13 weeks, the kid will have a defective heart.

Week 5 has a full-page picture of places the egg could implant outside the uterus—ectopic pregnancies. An ectopic pregnancy means the pregnancy has to be terminated and I could become infertile. One in 100 pregnancies land outside the uterus.

I am freaking out. I call Janet to thank her for the book. I say, "Um, this book is filled with dreadful possibilities."

"Oh, I know," she says. "I just like it for the pictures."

## Week 8

Today is my first appointment with an obstetrician. I am lying on the exam table with my feet in the stirrups. With one hand deep between my legs and the other pressing down on my belly—a pelvic exam—the doctor makes a very alarming face.

"What is it?"

"I'm not sure," she says. "I can't find the pregnancy."

With that, she leaves the room, leaving me in a slight panic, and returns minutes later with another doctor. The first doctor tells the second doctor she's concerned there's an ectopic pregnancy or possibly two uteruses.

"Two uteruses!" I say. "I've never heard of that."

The second doctor says calmly, "It's very rare. Let me take a look." She smiles and tells me what she's going to do. While she pats my knee with one hand, she puts two fingers of her gloved hand into my vagina. Right away she says, "This feels like a fibroid. Fibroids are very common."

All I can say is, "What?"

Then, with plenty of lubricant, she inserts a dildolike sonogram camera. She points to my uterus on the monitor and says: "Your uterus is tilted back. It will come forward as the pregnancy moves along. It looks to me like there's plenty of fluid, indicating a healthy pregnancy. This dark area here is the fibroid."

She sends me immediately to radiology to do a more sophisticated sonogram, just to be sure. They take me right away, which is both comforting and disconcerting.

In less than an hour, I take the X rays back to the second doctor, and they show what she predicted. My uterus tilts backward and I have a fibroid the size of a grapefruit.

I tell her about Robin. How she died of cancer six months

after giving birth. How Robin thought she had a fibroid. How furious I am at Robin's doctors for not finding the cancer sooner.

She listens, unhurried, and says she understands. She insists that fibroids are not dangerous and that most women have them and never know. She draws me a picture of my uterus and my fibroid, and I notice she is very pretty. She has freckles on her nose and a dimple when she smiles.

She lays out three scenarios: 1) the fibroid won't grow any more, 2) the fibroid will grow along with the fetus and cause pain, or 3) the fibroid will grow and not cause pain but may get in the way of the vagina during labor. None of the scenarios include cancer.

## Week 8, day 5

Everything smells like shit. This is a pregnancy side effect, some kind of prehistoric survival instinct to keep pregnant women from eating poison, but in modern society it's just disgusting. I can't sleep, because when I put my head down I am overwhelmed by the smell of Tea Rose, a sickeningly sweet perfume that reminds me of Dottie Lieberman, an old lady who lived upstairs from my grandparents in their condominium. When I was little, Mrs. Lieberman would kiss me and leave her scent on my face all day.

I gave away two bottles of conditioner in the last month, because I thought the smell was coming from my hair. But no matter what I used to wash my hair, I still smelled the same gross flowers. It had to be my place, so I started looking for a new apartment.

Then this morning I noticed a pink candle that has never been lit sitting on top of the bookcase about ten feet from my pillow. As I moved closer, the smell intensified. I grabbed it with a paper towel and threw it outside.

My sense of smell is so strong I can tell what kind of deodorant someone's wearing. This is a talent I wish I didn't have. The woman next door at work, Leah, wears Tom's of Maine. So natural it smells like rotting carrots. I can't go into her office anymore.

I call a friend I haven't spoken to in years. She just had a baby. Her baby is eight weeks old. "You have to get support," she says. "You're going to be more exhausted than you've ever been in your life. My feeding schedule is every three hours, day and night. You can't do it alone."

A few years ago, the first time Kate and I broke up, I told Robin I was serious about getting pregnant, and she said with such certainty, like she knew better than anyone, "You can't do it alone."

I didn't say anything. Our friendship wasn't what it was in high school, and we never fought to get it back.

Robin and I met in Spanish class on the first day of high school. We grew up in Miami, Florida, where heat and palm trees dictated fashion. Also, it was the mid-'80s, so I wore my new blue-and-white Puma sneakers, stonewashed jeans, and a white tank top. LIFEGUARD was printed in bold red letters across my chest. Robin wore pink shorts and a short-sleeved top that buttoned down the front. The outfit made Robin, who was naturally very thin, look extremely long. She was dorky—shy and smart, with not such good posture. She had very big brown eyes, perfect skin, and a pretty mouth: straight teeth and full lips. And a straight nose. Her ears stuck out through her shaggy, dirty-blond hair. When she was called on in class, she'd fluff up her hair above her ears, but they'd still poke through.

Robin was one of the smart kids; she never got a wrong answer. And without being obnoxious she spoke with a perfect Spanish accent.

Once, when I was called on and didn't know the answer,

I said: "That's too hard." No one ever admitted not knowing an answer, so the whole class burst out laughing. I had a laughing fit and got kicked out. On my way to the door, I glanced over at Robin, like she was my one emergency phone call. She sat attentively and gave me a knowing look as if to say, *Oh, silly Andrea.*

I worried she thought I was a nutball and I think a little bit she did. But I invited her anyway to go out to lunch with my friends, and even though she was decidedly not like us, she wasn't so different either. We were honor students who ran for student council. Robin soon became part of our crowd.

Robin and I loved to talk about how different we were from each other, how she was the smart one and I was the clown, but she was the one I wanted to talk to. Soon we became best friends, although we never said so. We had an understanding, and I didn't want to jinx it.

Robin was the first person I really talked to about feelings. We told each other what we were most insecure about, and as high school girls, we were insecure about lots of things. I worried that if I told Robin something scary, she wouldn't like me anymore. But she always did.

Robin told me she was afraid that something was wrong with her, because she didn't have a boyfriend. She would say, "But you love me, so I must be okay." Every time she wrote me a note and handed it to me in the hall between classes or first thing in the morning, I would love her more. I was in love with Robin in high school.

I must have been so afraid of being a lesbian, because the thought of being sexual with Robin never occurred to me. Instead I would get drunk and fool around with different guys I didn't care about. Robin was waiting for true love, or at least meaning. She was careful that way.

I didn't have intercourse; I did "everything but," the term my friends used for everything but intercourse, which was acceptable sexual behavior for a 17-year-old back then. Every time I did everything but, I'd tell Robin the details, which always felt more intimate than the actual event. I was embarrassed to tell her, but compelled to. And Robin would always say the same thing: "You're never happy after you fool around with a guy."

Several years later, when we'd both graduated from college and I had come out as a lesbian and Robin had gotten married, moved to the suburbs, and had her first child, I asked her if we would have been lovers during high school if we'd thought of it.

"Yes," she said, like it was no big deal.

We had been best friends for three years. It was the middle of our senior year and the whole school was waiting for SAT scores to come in the mail. I walked barefoot down my rocky driveway one Saturday afternoon in February 1986. It was hot, even for Miami. The mail was late, and I was anxious and sweaty in the pits. I had everything I needed: grades, sports, extracurricular activities, even volunteer work. I just needed high SATs. The SATs would decide my fate for the rest of my life. Either I'd get into a good college or I'd be one of the dumb kids.

The envelope was in the mailbox. I sat down on the grass at the end of my driveway and opened it. Verbal: 480. Math: 610. 1090. That's it?

Robin called, and I told her I was too depressed to go out. She said, "Please come over; we'll stay home and talk."

I told her I couldn't move, so she came over to my house, and we sat on my bed for hours. She got a 1450 and I was truly happy for her. I actually thought she'd get a perfect 1600, but still she was in anywhere she wanted to go.

"I'm not smart," I said.

"They're not that bad," she said. I felt a huge lump rise

up in my throat. I couldn't even look at her. As much as I resisted, I started to cry. I cried hard. She put a tape of Phil Collins into my boom box and brought it to the bed. I leaned against a pillow, and Robin leaned against me. She rewound after *You're Taking It All Too Hard,* and we listened to that song ten times in a row.

"I thought I was smart."

"You are smart," Robin said. "I mean it, I wouldn't be friends with you if you weren't smart."

It got late and we got under the covers. She said, "I've never seen you cry before."

"I'm lucky," I said. "Nothing has ever been this sad." She hugged me and kept her arm around me while we fell asleep.

A few months later, our friendship started to crack. Robin got in early admission to the University of Pennsylvania. I applied also and was waiting to hear.

But Penn was Robin's school. According to Robin, I wasn't supposed to go to Penn. I know this because she let it slip. We were standing behind the counter at Love that Yogurt, our after-school job at the mall. That day was slow, and when business was slow we'd lean over the counter and count how many people we knew. We'd keep score. You had to spot the person first and know his or her full name to get a point. Or you'd get a point if someone said your name. All of our friends had jobs at the mall and anyone from our school could be there on any day. I always got more points than she did.

Robin spotted Jeremy Pines, a kid from her AP History class. I didn't know him. Robin said, "Jeremy applied to Penn. He had no business applying. He only got 1200 on his SATs."

I felt sick suddenly, like I had taken a swig of rotten milk. Jeremy Pines scored 110 points higher than I did. Robin knew

I applied to Penn. Robin knew how devastated and insecure I was about my SAT score. She was the only person I cried in front of over it. She was the only person, except my mom, I remembered ever crying in front of over anything.

I couldn't speak. I went to the back of the store to cut strawberries. Robin stayed in the front and restocked the candy bins.

A year later, when we were both home from Penn for the summer, a big group of our old high school friends went out to dinner. I told the hostess that we'd like to sit outside. Robin said, loud enough for me to hear, but not directly to me and in a tone that was not praising, "Andrea always tries to get what she wants."

Robin may not have meant to hurt me, but I felt the same shame and anger I felt that day behind the counter at Love that Yogurt. It was just like Robin to take a backhanded jab at me without the courage to clearly say what she felt—not like Kate, who would tell me to my face every time something I did hurt her feelings.

Robin and I never fought; it just wasn't part of our relationship. Instead, weirdness developed between us that we never discussed. I didn't say, "Fuck you for implying that I'm not smart enough for Penn." I didn't say, "What do you mean, I always try to get what I want? Would I try to get what I don't want?"

And when she said I couldn't have a baby alone, I didn't say what had been building for years: *Damn you for not believing in me, and damn you for taking such a conventional road.*

## Week 9

I notice one good side effect of being pregnant. But now I can't remember what it is.

Memory loss is one of the side effects. The books call it

"pregnancy brain." The books also call consistent nausea day and night "morning sickness." I get morning sickness at 5 in the afternoon. Walking makes me throw up on the sidewalk.

I am kneeling at the side of the road when a bicyclist goes by. I feel embarrassed and try to quell the heaving. The bicyclist turns out to be Andrea Stern, a good friend and neighbor, which embarrasses me even more.

I smile and try to play it off like nothing is out of the ordinary. Extreme self-consciousness is also a side effect.

Andrea stops and says hello. She tells me she thought I was praying.

No, I stopped praying a week after that day in fifth grade when I found a lump on my chest under my left nipple while doing the Pledge of Allegiance. I prayed religiously for a week: "Please, God, I'll keep my room clean. I'll do the dishes every night. Whatever you want, just please don't let me grow boobs."

I told Susie Blizzard, my friend who lived next door, that I was going to have to go to the hospital to get a lump removed. I said it like I was going camping or doing something fun. I don't remember being afraid of cancer, although the possibility did occur to me. More likely I thought I had a cyst. My brother had one on the back of his knee and all he had to do was have an operation and eat ice cream. Right then, in fifth grade, cancer beat growing boobs.

A week later, my mom took me to the pediatrician and I found out what was wrong with me. Dr. Feinberg rubbed his big cold hands together and put one under my shirt. He rolled his fingers over the "troubling spot," as he called it, and then rolled his fingers over the other side. "You've got nothing to worry about, Kiddo. This is development."

God failed me.

I've learned the difference between nauseous and nauseated. I've had to, the conversation comes up so often. Most people use the words incorrectly. The fact is, pregnancy makes me nauseated, which means it makes me feel like throwing up. Pregnancy is also a nauseous condition, which means it makes me feel like throwing up.

When someone says, "I'm so nauseous," she's really saying that she exhibits qualities that will make someone else throw up. The sound of the word itself is nauseating. It's best not to talk about it, but I find myself explaining over and over the sick, burning feeling in my gut that goes away only for ten minutes while I'm eating.

## Week 9, day 2

My heart is beating fast, like I'm panicking. My baby's heart is beating fast too, faster than you can tap your finger. I saw it on the ultrasound monitor. Made me smile. The baby's heart is supposed to beat fast. Mine's not.

I have not been able to open my jaws wide for three weeks. It hurts to chew. My therapist told me this is fight or flight. I am in a constant state of terror.

I am afraid of how afraid I feel.

I tell my friends to stay away. I'm distracted and can't make conversation. I can't ask, How are you?, because then I have to listen to the answer. Conversation is too exhausting.

Stephanie begs to make dinner for me. She'll sleep over and make breakfast too. This sounds like a nice offer, since cooking is such a chore and eating is the only relief I have from the nausea.

I tell her, No, thank you, and she practically cries. "I want to be there for you," she says.

I say, "Steph, I can't be around you. I have to fart." Gas is another side effect. "You can be there by leaving me alone."

She says, "I've been afraid that when you have a baby, it

won't be the two of us anymore. But I already miss you."

I know she's being sweet and that she loves me and that I am being impossible. And before I got pregnant I feared I would lose the closeness of my friends without kids. Right now, I never want to talk to her again.

I wake up in the middle of the night, freaking out. Like tonight it hurts in my lower belly on the left side. What is that bulge? Maybe it's the fibroid. Why didn't they notice it before I got pregnant? One in 200 fibroids are malignant. Robin's dead.

Is this cancer?

I can't get comfortable. I'm lying awake at 3 A.M. afraid I'm having a miscarriage. I wish I could be like Carolyn Finger's mother. She didn't notice she was pregnant until six months, when Carolyn kicked. She thought she was starting menopause. She was off by 16 years.

I take a bath to try to relax. The books say baths in the first trimester are okay as long as the temperature doesn't go above 98 degrees. The bath feels perfect, warm but not too hot. But to be safe I take out my basal body thermometer, the one I used to track my menstrual cycle, and measure the bath's temperature: 103 degrees. I'm sure now, at 3:45 A.M., that I've boiled my baby.

### WEEK 9, DAY 3

I wake up at 8 in the morning, nauseated. What a relief, I'm still pregnant.

### WEEK 9, DAY 5

I'm cracking. I've lost my gauge for hungry and full. I'm eating so much. I'm a cow. It's 9 P.M., and I'm curled up on the couch alone. I eat cookies and go to bed.

I am up at 3 in the morning for the fifth night in a row. I dreamt about Robin, only in the dream she looked like Kate. We were sitting together in my parents' bed in the middle of the night after a high school party. My parents were out of town. Other kids were passed out on couches or on the floor around the house, but we got the best bed. There was an understanding between us that we didn't have much time left together, but we didn't talk about it.

She said she was really happy to be spending the night with me. We kissed a little. I kept saying, "I love you." Telling her felt so satisfying, but I also felt the loss. She wanted me to touch her, so I did, really gently and hesitantly. I was afraid to love her fully.

## WEEK 9, DAY 6
No one says feeling miserable is a side effect. Everyone talks about pregnancy bliss and the prenatal glow. This is the worst experience of my life. When people ask, How are you? I say, "I've never felt worse." I'm antisocial, fat, and scared.

## WEEK 9, DAY 7
My grandpa died today. He was 89. My dad calls to tell me. He misses him, but says it's the right order of things. "He enjoyed his life," my dad says.

My grandpa died quickly, without too much suffering, from lung cancer. He had survived lung cancer twice in his life, after 50 years of smoking. He quit 25 years ago.

I spoke to my grandpa, my favorite man in the world next to my brother, for the last time four days ago. He took my call even though he had barely any energy to speak. I said, "You're my number one."

He said, "You're my number one."

My grandpa had said that to me my whole life, even in

front of my brother. He'd laugh and tell Tony he was his number one and a half.

Two weeks ago, he spent several days in the hospital before the doctors figured out the cancer had moved to his throat. When we spoke, his voice was weak and hoarse. He didn't carry on like he usually did the other times in his life when he was in the hospital. He didn't say: "A person could go crazy in here. A day in here feels like a week."

Instead, he said, "They found the cancer in my throat."

"Is the cancer going to kill you?" I asked, because I thought cancer moved slowly in older people.

He said, "I'm ninety years old."

"You're eighty-nine."

"When you're ninety, something's gonna get you."

"Are you scared?"

"My life's been good," he said.

I make a plane reservation to Miami for tomorrow. I call my grandma. She is calm. "He was suffering," she says.

"Not for very long," I say.

"Oh, he was in so much pain."

My grandma lost her husband of 70 years. It must have been difficult to see him hurting, especially because he never admitted to pain. After falling off a moped he said he was fine, only he didn't lift his arm for days. Finally, he got an Xray, and his collarbone was broken.

I talk to my mom. She loved him. Even though my parents have split up, he was her father-in-law for 36 years. She cries. I talk to Tony. He is sad but thinking practically. Who will take care of Grandma? Who will drive her to the grocery store?

I feel very close to my family, even if I am 3,000 miles away. We're in this together.

## WEEK 10

I am on my way to Miami to bury my grandpa. No more driving around in his Chevy Bel Air looking at Christmas lights. No more ice cream that falls off its cone. No more being called Miss Dropsy. No more sitting on his lap going down the big slide at the fair. I haven't done those things in 30 years, but now I miss them.

It feels good to think about my grandpa. Strangely, it's a relief to think about something that is truly sad.

·

## WEEK 10, DAY 2

Today is my grandpa's funeral and Robin's birthday. She would have been 35. The rabbi I grew up with meets us at the cemetery. He is warm, and I've always liked him. I tell him I'm pregnant, and he hugs me. He doesn't ask who the father is or how I got pregnant or if I have a partner. I consider saying *I'm a single lesbian and was artificially inseminated, in case you were wondering*. But I tell him today is Robin's birthday, and we talk about the two of us in confirmation class. He remembers the time I wore slippers in the sanctuary. I tell him I'm sorry I did that; that was disrespectful. He says, "You were a funny kid."

As we walk toward my grandpa's burial spot, I ask the rabbi about circumcision. I have been wondering lately, in case I have a boy, what's really the point. The rabbi, who leads a Reform synagogue and is politically liberal, says that circumcision ensures that a man will think about God when he has sex. "Sex becomes not only an act of love with someone else, but also with God."

He said *with someone else*. He could have easily said *with a woman*. Maybe he knows I'm a lesbian.

I see Janet and rush over to her. Her belly is popping out, she is showing, and she looks adorable. Her hair is curly and crazier than usual and her big red lips look perfectly kissable.

I kiss her on the lips and thank her for coming. "Let's stop meeting at funerals," I say. It has been a year and a half since Robin's, but it feels like last week.

I ask Janet if the rabbi knows I'm a lesbian. "He's never mentioned anything to me," she says.

We gather around the gravesite, and my brother welcomes everybody. He looks down at a piece of notebook paper he has prepared to lead today's service. The rabbi says a prayer, but Tony is the rabbi today. I am so proud of my brother, who was once so skinny and shy. My dad speaks and so does my uncle. Then I get up to speak.

I feel nervous and sad. I begin by saying, "I'm ten weeks pregnant." Most of my extended family and friends of my family don't know. Most of them have known me all my life and may or may not know I'm a lesbian. My parents have never told anyone, not even their own siblings. So when I told their siblings, one by one, they were surprised. The silence has hurt me over the years. It always made me feel like my parents thought something was wrong with me.

I continue: "I feel connected to the past, my grandpa, and the future, my baby. I want my baby to inherit the qualities I loved in my grandpa. I hope he or she is down-to-earth and street-smart. I hope she loves food and says, 'Best you've ever tasted!' I hope he has strong opinions and expresses them loudly. I hope she likes playing with children and is committed to family. I hope he's funny. I hope she enjoys getting older."

Tony speaks last and makes this a happy funeral as funerals go, just as my grandpa would have wanted. He tells a story about my grandpa, at 85, climbing a ladder to fix his roof. He wanted to save money, so he thought he'd fix it himself. When Tony found out, he scolded him. My grandpa said, "Don't worry, Grandma was holding the ladder."

In the car on the way home my mom says, "Why did you use the eulogy as an opportunity to announce you were pregnant?"

"Because it helped me explain how I feel about Grandpa. What's wrong with that?"

"Nothing, I suppose. Nothing."

"What?"

"The eulogy was all about you."

"Everybody's eulogy was about them." I sit and stew for a half hour while Bob drives us home. It occurs to me that she is still embarrassed about her lesbian daughter.

When I came out 13 years ago, I was shocked by my parents' reaction. I thought both my parents were liberal and open-minded. My dad is extremely easygoing: He never wears a tie. He takes a nap every day. He gives generously to charity. And my mom was on the board of the local National Organization for Women. She regularly stood on the street with her friends, including lesbians, protesting for equal pay for equal work or a woman's right to choose an abortion. I think she even marched in Gay Pride. My mom was a women's libber.

And I thought I had their unconditional love.

My mom was always my confidante. I could tell her everything, and did. I told her I was going to have sex for the first time, when I was dating guys, because I thought if I couldn't tell my mom, I wasn't really ready. She said, "Is there anything you'd like to know about how to do it?"

"No, thanks, Mom," I said.

My dad was my champion. He thought I could be the best tennis player in the world, if I wanted. He also thought I could be a brain surgeon, if that's what I wanted.

My brother and I grew up listening to Marlo Thomas and Alan Alda, the progressive stars of the '70s, who made a record called *Free to Be You and Me*: "Don't dress your cat in an apron, just 'cause he's learning to bake.... A person can wear what she wants to, no matter what other folks say. A person can be what he wants to, a person's a person that way." I believed that record.

I had made love for the first time five days before coming out to my parents. In junior high, when my friends put posters of Sean Cassidy on their walls and wrote boys' names on their notebooks, I didn't get it. Finally, I understood what a crush meant, and then my crush came to fruition. She wore lipstick and black clothes and was a novelist in New York City, where I was living at the time.

With both my parents on the phone, I said, "I'm in a relationship...with a woman."

"This is not what we want for you," my mom said. Then she cried. "You're choosing another mother."

"No one will ever take your place," I said.

I know that my mom reveres Mother. She considers the mother the ultimate caretaker and motherly love the most devoted love. I said, "If it's true that I'm choosing another mother, a second mother, don't we all want that? Don't you want that for me?" She didn't answer.

She was jealous and I think also embarrassed because maybe my lesbianism implicated her as a lesbian. She thought it was her fault. She said she led me to it by encouraging me to volunteer, the summer before, for a congressional campaign staffed by lesbians. But I think her biggest fear was that I would never have a baby. "I want to be a mom," I said.

My dad thought telling anyone would sabotage any chance I had left of getting together with a man. He said, "Who have you told?"

"I told Stephanie and Robin and Janet and Todd and the man at the Mini Mart and..."

I have spent the last 13 years trying to get my family back, especially my mom.

Maybe my mom thinks announcing I'm pregnant without a husband reveals that I'm a lesbian. We're home now, and I get out of the car and slam the door. "You're still homophobic," I say.

She follows behind me as I walk quickly to the house. "I am not. It's not what I want for you, but I have nothing against gay people. I don't want you to be black; that doesn't mean I'm a racist. I don't want you to have polio; that doesn't mean I have something against people with polio. I don't think it's nice for you to say that."

## Week 10, day 4

I'm back in Los Angeles and Kate takes me out to dinner, because my birthday's tomorrow. I haven't seen her since I got pregnant. I feel relieved to spend time with her. No one knows me better. I can fart with Kate.

We sit down at our favorite restaurant, Chaya Venice, where we went so many times for their $12, late-night sushi bowl, and tears sneak out of my eyes and down my cheeks. Talking to Kate about being pregnant breaks my heart all over again. I don't wish in this moment to be together, but I am aware that we are not.

Kate is gentle with me and holds my hand as she walks me to my car. She tells me the woman she's dating doesn't like public affection, and that makes her miss me. Kate is still mine. We hug, and it is so familiar. A perfect fit: I am the hot dog and she is the bun.

I drive home crying so hard driving is dangerous. I have to pull over a few times to wipe off my glasses. I call Kate when I get home. I say, "Thank you for being the person who opens me up and lets me cry."

"Listen," she says. "You have to call other people when you're upset. I am not that person for you anymore."

"What? Why can't you just say, 'Thank you'? I'm not

saying you're my girlfriend. I'm just saying you're special. You're my family."

"You have to find other support."

## WEEK 10, DAY 6

Ravi and I planned a birthday party together at my place, but I canceled it. Ravi's on the board of directors of Bike Out, the organization I founded and directed for the last five years, and he has taken a liking to me. He's gay and fun and loves to talk about sex, and his birthday is the day before mine. We've been working closely together for the past year, fighting a lot and then making up. He's a pain in the ass, because he thinks he knows everything and everybody. I see that now I'm a pain in the ass too, but I couldn't have the party. I didn't want to see people. I didn't want to celebrate anything, especially not myself. I hate myself. I'm sure Ravi hates me too, because he's already sent out invitations.

On my 35th birthday I eat cereal for dinner, talk to my mom, and go to bed.

## WEEK 11

I know I have to eat well, but cooking for one depresses me, so I invite Andrea Stern over for dinner. I make chicken, mashed potatoes, and a spinach salad. We chat and eat and then Andrea sits on the couch and finishes her beer. She dials a number on her cell phone while I clear the table. She doesn't even put the butter away.

"You could help clean up," I say.

She thinks I'm kidding. She smiles and says, "Hold on." I have interrupted her.

I say, "Don't get on the phone while we're hanging out."

"I'm just checking my messages," she says.

"That's rude."

When she finishes, she says, "Are you really mad?"

"Yes. And you could help clean up. I just spent an hour cooking." She still thinks I'm kidding and puts her feet up on the coffee table.

"I was just seeing if Juliet was free tonight, because I was also wondering if you wanted to go to a movie later."

"Please. Don't tell me you're checking to see if there's anything better to do first."

"What's your problem?"

I do the dishes, and then I tell her I don't want to go to a movie. I want her to leave.

## WEEK 11, DAY 2

Everyone's sending me maternity clothes. I know they mean well, but it's got to stop. My sister-in-law, Lisa, who lives in the suburbs of Miami with my brother and three kids and a dog and a cat and lots of white tile and wood laminate floors and the air-conditioner running year round, sent me a huge bag of her old outfits: black-and-white polka-dotted frocks. They all have built-in boobs and ribbons that tie in the back with a bow. They are so ugly, a cross between matron and little girl. These are clothes for a PTA mother.

Today, Janet sends me an outfit from the maternity section of Old Navy—a knee-length denim skirt with a kangaroo pouch in front. The skirt is so ugly I shove it back in the box.

This must be a plot to turn me into a straight, suburban mom. They want me to be just like them. Just because I'm pregnant doesn't mean I'm not still a lesbian.

Andrea Stern calls just to chat. She doesn't have anything to say; she just wants company. "Don't call me just to lag on the phone," I say. "Only call me if you specifically want to talk to me."

She says, "Wow, you're not right. Good-bye."

## WEEK 11, DAY 3

Stephanie calls me at work. She doesn't try to see me, but offers an intervention. She said she spoke to Andrea Stern, and they're starting to worry. "Call my old therapist," she says. "You need help."

She gives me the number and says, "Call right now. I'll call you back in ten minutes."

I do need help, and the therapist I'm currently seeing isn't helping. I call. I say, "I'm eleven weeks pregnant and have never felt so depressed."

She says, "You have hormone-induced depression."

I say, "I know, that's why I'm calling you."

"Well, we could talk for days and nothing would help. You need to talk to your gynecologist or a psychiatrist who specializes in pregnancy."

This reminds me of the time I experienced my first real heartbreak after breaking up with my first girlfriend and had diarrhea for two months. I went to a colon specialist and told him I was having loose bowels. He did a very intrusive test of my anus and colon—pretty much stuck a movie camera up my butt—and then said, "You have Irritable Bowel."

I said, "I know, that's why I'm seeing you."

Stephanie calls me back.

"No one can help me," I say.

## WEEK 11, DAY 5

The only friends I can stand, for some reason, are Dave and Cynthia. They don't need entertaining, and they don't seem to care that I'm in a bad mood. Maybe they do care, and I don't notice, because it's just my attempt to hold on to Kate. Kate and Dave were lovers in college and Cynthia was Kate's college roommate. Now Dave and Cynthia are married and are still Kate's best friends. They were our best friends when we were a couple and we'd barbecue every other weekend.

Dave and Cynthia would come over and make jerk chicken and sausages while I made guacamole and Kate drank beer. They didn't expect Kate to help. They knew her too well.

Dave is very tactile. He loves soft things, and until Kate would shoo him away, he'd play with her earlobes or the skin on her elbows. Sometimes he'd hold on to her arm, squeezing gently, seemingly unconsciously. I understand Dave's compulsion. Kate feels like kittens and marshmallows.

Dave acted like a kid around Kate. They'd argue heatedly about the value of art versus service in society, and two seconds later Dave would try to lift her shirt to get a pat on her belly. He called her breasts "fund-raisers," and talked about ways she could use them for charity: "Like a kissing booth, you could pull those babies out and collect money in your bra." Kate and Cynthia would roll their eyes.

I'd say, "Great idea," and plot with Dave. We loved being pigs.

Seeing Dave and Kate together always warmed my heart and also made me sad. Sure, Dave hadn't lived with Kate in 15 years, but I couldn't love her as easily and as unconditionally as Dave seemed to.

We have a picnic on Memorial Day. I tell Cynthia I have a newfound love of cheese, and she makes me a mozzarella sandwich. The day is nice, but without Kate, I have a bad feeling, like I've lost my wallet.

## WEEK 12, DAY 2

I'm having trouble swallowing my prenatal vitamins. They're as big as horse pills. They get to the back of my throat and then I gag. Today I tried cutting one in half, but that just doubled the agony. I need chewable prenatal vitamins.

I'm the biggest baby. I'm remembering watching Robin take her medication, and now I'm disgusted with myself.

A month after they found the cancer and just five months before she died, I went to visit Robin in New Jersey. Before I left California, I was shaky nervous. My dad told me to ask her how she feels and to talk about the cancer. He said, "Remember how afraid you were to graduate high school?" I didn't want to move away and leave my friends. "Well, wasn't the actual event a lot easier than worrying about it? You'll be fine."

I arrived late at night. Robin had left a key in the mailbox and the bed made up in the guestroom.

I was up early the next morning, eager to see her. Her whole family—mom, dad, husband, newborn, 3-year-old, and Robin's uncle—and I were in the kitchen waiting.

Finally, Robin appeared. I raised my arms and cheered. From a distance she looked exactly like she did in high school. I rushed over. We hugged. I was careful. Robin had just had a baby, but she was so thin. Way too thin. She was still so pretty.

We sat down next to each other at the table. Robin looked straight ahead. I saw hair under her chin and on her neck. It wasn't thick, but long and soft-looking. She had told me over the phone that this might happen. Her body was no longer producing estrogen.

"I'm ready for my poached eggs, please," Robin said to her dad.

"One or two?"

"Two, please."

Her mom sat down at the breakfast table, and we talked about Lance Armstrong, who was in the newspaper and about to win another Tour de France. Her mom said Lance beat cancer, and I finally took a full breath. We were talking about cancer.

Robin ate almost all of her poached eggs and whole wheat toast. I was sure her mom and dad were watching her eat as carefully as I was.

"Sophie, help me take my vitamins," Robin said, in the sweetest, most inviting mommy voice. Sophia came over and popped up onto her lap. Robin held several pills in her thin, capable hand. "Which one first?"

Sophia said: "Red." Robin took it. Then black. Then the half blue. The whole blue. The two whites.

There was one green pill left. Robin said, "Okay, now the purple."

"That's not purple," Sophia said. She laughed. Robin laughed too.

After breakfast, Robin moved to the couch. "I have to rest after all that morning activity," she said, trying to be light. Then seriously, "I feel better when the medication kicks in."

## Week 12, day 3

I see my pretty doctor, Dr. Elena Martinez. It's been four weeks since we've seen each other. I'm thinking, I need her more than ever, but I don't want to come across too desperate.

Stephanie comes with me for added support and to see the baby on the ultrasound. She edges in next to me on the bed to see the monitor, and I wonder if Dr. Martinez thinks Stephanie's my lover. I don't clarify. Sometimes I wish she were.

The monitor shows a picture of the moon, but I think I can make out the baby. I think I see the butt. The legs are dangling down. "Looks like a girl," I say.

"It's still too soon to tell," Dr. Martinez says.

"Oh no, it's a boy?" I ask. Now I'm thinking that with her professional experience she can tell it's a boy, she just doesn't want to give it away. She smiles at me as if she knows me well, and even though she doesn't, it feels good.

I tell the doctor I'm not myself and that I've never been so miserable in my life, and she says I can take Prozac if I want to. I think about those pregnant women in the '50s who took drugs to relieve morning sickness. Doctors must have told them Thalidomide was safe. Their children were born without hands and feet. They had flippers instead.

I don't want to take Prozac. But then, am I hurting my baby because he or she is awash in negativity, in depression chemicals? Robin's body was ravaged with cancer while she was pregnant, and her baby was born healthy. My theory is that this baby is sucking up whatever it needs, and I am left depleted. At 12 weeks, my baby measures in at 13 weeks on the ultrasound. My baby is big and happy.

I show the doctor my stomach. I say, "Is this right?" I look so pregnant it startles me.

She says, "The fibroid is probably making your stomach more distended."

I ask about the weight gain, and she says 12 pounds *is* a lot at this stage. I blush uncontrollably. My heart is beating so fast again. I am entirely conscious of how self-conscious I am. Dr. Martinez must notice, because she starts making excuses for me: "Don't worry, this is a new scale, and you're wearing heavy sneakers."

Oh my god, I'm fat.

Stephanie says, "Think of your body not as the athlete's body it used to be, but as a life creator." I take that to mean I'm fat.

# Before Pregnancy

Kate said that the day I turned 30 I started to talk, a lot, about having a baby. The minute my brother called to say Lisa was in labor with their second child, I rushed to the airport and flew home. I got an afternoon flight without telling anyone I was coming, and made it to the hospital by 9 P.M., five hours after Danielle was born. I carried my backpack and a woven bassinet—a giant straw basket I'd gotten at the Farmer's Market—and rushed toward the nursery, where Tony was standing in front of the glass, holding Big Sister Rachel, who was almost 3. He must have sensed I was coming because as soon as I rounded the corner and spotted him down the long, quiet hallway he looked my way and screamed, "My sister!"

The nurse wheeled the baby into Lisa's room, and the four of us spent hours watching the new baby, Danielle. I didn't want to leave those girls and realized then that I wanted one of my own.

My parents had also just split up after 36 years.

Kate and I had been together for two years, and with the birth of my nieces and the breakup of my family, I created a fantasy and clung hard to it. Kate and I would have babies together and have our own family.

A perfect date was an evening at the grocery store and the two of us making dinner together. The only problem was that Kate hated the grocery store and always wanted to go out to dinner.

At that time, five years ago, Kate was pursuing a journalism career at the *Los Angeles Times,* and I was creating a nonprofit organization. I had been out of a job for almost a year. I had gotten the ax from U.S. PIRG, a grungy, grassroots environmental group. I was their national Right to Know campaign coordinator, which meant I lobbied for the right to know what toxic chemicals were polluting our world, except I couldn't remember the names of the chemicals I was tracking. Names like polyzorbitalulene, cosmic-butane, and methyl ethyl death. Something like that. One time, I organized a press conference and said on TV: "BASF is spewing poison from their smokestacks and making U.S. citizens sick." I thought it was a pretty great sound bite, but I learned later that you have to be precise when accusing companies of expelling such unpleasantries, or your organization could be charged with libel. I guess I didn't have the savvy for this kind of work.

After that job, I sat at my desk, in my bedroom, where I'd been sitting for months, getting up for a daily bike ride and then back to my desk. My career as an environmentalist was shot, but I was building my new career, as a freelance writer. I was sending out story ideas to magazines. I was writing a novel. I had just finished a spec script for a TV show, and was hard at work on a restaurant review column for a local weekly newspaper. The problem was I only got paid $25 and a free meal a week.

Kate came home from work and stood at the door to our room. I had just asked her how you spell *focaccia* when she said, "I don't know if I can date someone like you. The only thing you do consistently is ride your bike. I need to date a lawyer."

I got right on my bike feeling accused of not being smart enough. Kate didn't respect my food column. She knew I didn't know anything about food and said I was writing advertisements for restaurants. Yes, it was shoddy journalism, and she was the real thing, but I needed to start somewhere. Kate thought I was resting on old laurels, like a washed-up high school football hero. She thought I was that slacker uncle in everyone's family who tries everything but amounts to nothing.

That was the part that hurt the most, because at that moment, it appeared to be true. My overachieving came and went. In elementary school, I was captain of the pep club and a safety patrol. In junior high, nothing. In high school, I was named scholar athlete. In college, academic probation. After college, at just 22 years old, I created the Reproductive Freedom Ride. I raised $30,000 and led 11 people across the country on our bicycles. We became local television news stars, rallying in towns along the way, demanding sex education, access to abortion, universal health care, and equality for gay families.

But right then, when Kate said she needed to date a lawyer—someone who had finished law school and passed the bar and had a real job and who took an interest in world affairs and would debate probable cause after sex—I was unemployed and underachieving. Shit, Kate was right. All I wanted to do was ride my bike.

As I biked north along the Pacific Coast Highway into

Malibu, I thought: How can I make a life of this? I want to make a difference in the world, but I also want to ride my bike.

Stephanie and I went for a bike ride the next day. I said, "I've got it. I'm creating a biking organization for inner-city kids. It's called Bike Out. Get it? Bike out, like outside?" I explained how we'd go into the mountains with just our bikes and food for a week. How we'd camp and survive in the wilderness and how the kids would learn what they're really made of.

Steph loved the idea. "That'll take tremendous effort, but if anyone can do it, you can," she said. She was always my biggest fan.

"Thanks. The only problem," I said. "It's not political enough for me." Inner-city kids needed help, I knew, but I wanted to feel personally connected to the cause, and I grew up upper-middle-class in the suburbs.

Steph said, "Do it for gay kids."

Kate and I were busy in our work. We were career women, and I was creating something important. But in the back of my mind I wanted to be ready for motherhood by 35, when doctors say fertility becomes compromised. So we began a five-year conversation about having a baby. Kate wanted to give birth to a child too. Because I was four years older, I would go first.

I wanted to know our donor. Kate wasn't so sure. I thought getting sperm from a bank to make a baby was bizarre, something out of a freaky newspaper story, like when the first test-tube baby was conceived. I didn't want my baby being part of that strange beginning.

I would want to know where I came from. Even the simple things like whose hands or whose eye shape I have are important to me. I like being able to trace these qualities. I feel part of a larger history—my family's history.

So I created a menu listing the pros and cons of some of our known-donor options to help us decide.

Option one: The Harvard Method. Kate coined the term, meaning we'd go to Harvard, I'd hang out in the library pretending to be a grad student, I'd seduce a freshman, have sex, get pregnant, and then skip town without telling him.

The Harvard Method pros: 1) Smart sperm, and 2) If he was a virgin, we could safely assume he didn't have any sexually transmitted diseases.

The Harvard Method cons: 1) No one's a virgin in college anymore, 2) Lying would create bad karma for our baby, and 3) We don't live in Boston.

Option two: The Fuck Me Method. I coined the term, meaning I would ask a guy to fuck me. Kate really didn't like this idea. Still, we started seeing men in a different light. I'd meet a good-looking one at a party and ask his height, his political opinions, what he did for work, for fun, did he get along with his parents, what did he get on the SATs. I would overhear Kate doing the same thing when she met a potential candidate.

The Fuck Me Method pros: 1) Seems like it would be easy to get a guy to say yes, since a few of my male friends have already said things like "I'll get you pregnant if I can deliver, heh, heh," and 2) Fresh sperm is known to be more effective.

The Fuck Me Method cons: 1) Kate hates the idea, and 2) We don't want a man that closely involved in our lives.

Option three: The Cowboy Method. I don't know who coined this term, but I think it's known in insemination circles. The Cowboy Method is fresh sperm produced by a man (I imagine him alone in a bathroom wearing a cowboy hat) into a jar (boiled in water, no detergent, because detergent may have sperm-killing agents), then handed over to the woman—or better, an intermediary (like a lover—who brings the sperm to the woman—who waits, propped upside down in her bedroom (I imagine candles and soft music). The sperm is then inserted with a syringe into the vagina.

The Cowboy Method pros: 1) I don't have to have sex with anyone besides Kate, and 2) Fresh sperm.

The Cowboy Method cons: 1) The man has to be on call whenever I ovulate, and 2) We can't be sure the sperm is disease-free.

Option four: The Deposit and Withdrawal Method. I coined this term, meaning a man I choose deposits sperm at a bank, to be used when I ovulate. The initial cost is $175 to test for motility, potency, STDs, and HIV. The sperm is then quarantined for six months. The final cost is $2,000 to freeze and store.

The Deposit and Withdrawal Method pros: 1) No man is present when I'm inseminated, 2) The sperm is tested and safe, and 3) Kate likes this option best.

The Deposit and Withdrawal Method cons: 1) Expensive, 2) I'll have to get pregnant in a doctor's office, and 3) There's a six-month wait before getting started.


There were other problems with all of the options. Mainly, the legal advice states the importance of creating a scenario in which the intentions of the donor are clear. Having sex with a man, for example, may muddy the line between donor and father. Even the appearance of fatherhood could create legal trouble if the donor wanted paternity rights.

The National Center for Lesbian Rights provides sample legal contracts to be signed by the donor and mother, but at that point it was unknown whether these documents would hold up in court.

Most of my friends warned against knowing the donor. But since I felt so strongly that I wanted to know him, I forged ahead. I soon learned it's impossible for a lesbian to find a good man.

Strike One: Janet's husband, Rob. Janet asked Rob to give me sperm because she was so excited about the possibility of me having a baby as sweet and cute as her little girl. She said, "If I could give you sperm, I would. No one wants to be pregnant more than you do."

Rob said, "I would be too attached to a child I helped conceive."

Janet said, "Think of it as giving money."

Strike Two: a friend named Mario. I asked Mario, a bicycle advocate from the Philippines, who is handsome and very sweet. He laughed hard when I asked him. I think he was surprised. He has a son and told me he wanted more children but that his wife can't conceive anymore. Oh no. I told him I would want him to have a limited role, like an uncle. He said okay. I said I was wary of having a mixed-race kid, because I'm not part of Filipino culture. He said Filipinos are already a mixed race. I felt better. Then I felt worse, since I knew nothing about the Philippines.

Kate and I talked a lot about a mixed-race kid. What is race, anyway, but a cultural construct based on skin color? We entertained the idea of a rainbow coalition of children: She'd get pregnant next with Indian sperm, then we'd adopt a little orphan girl from China and a boy from Africa.

In the end we decided that as much as we would want to celebrate Filipino holidays, learn to cook Filipino food, and vacation in the Philippines, we wouldn't be able to adequately provide Filipino culture, and that wouldn't be fair to our child. Our world is racist. And racial and cultural identity are still important, even to us. We would be a Jewish, lesbian family. That would be enough.

Strike Three: Kate's brother Dan. During a visit with Kate's family, Dan said on his own, without being asked, "If you want to have a baby, I'll donate sperm."

I smiled so big. He was completely sincere and not sleazy. I said, "What could be more perfect?" Dan is tall and good-looking and very smart. He's one of the nicest guys I know, and he is the closest Kate and I could come to having a child of our own.

Later, I got dreamy saying that using Dan's sperm could make a blond, blue-eyed child like her, with curly hair like me, and the kid would be really smart like her, with a positive disposition like me. Our child would actually be biologically related to both of us. I suggested getting my brother's sperm for Kate so our children would come from the same genes.

Kate argued it would create an unnatural closeness between her brother and me. She thought about the complications we'd have explaining Uncle Dan's relationship to our child. She didn't want an unseverable connection to our donor.

Kate was like that: always seeing the downside. I said, "This is your theme song," and sang Paul Simon's "Something So Right": " 'When something goes right, it's likely to lose me. It's apt to confuse me. It's such an unusual sight.' "

Out of curiosity, I called my brother to ask if he would give us sperm for Kate. He said no.

## 9 MONTHS (BP)

I found a good man: a man who understood my vision and would join me in creating a life; one who was good-looking and smart and happy-go-lucky; a gay guy who wanted to have a role in the child's life, but would be hands-off about day-to-day parenting.

I had spotted Erik three years ago, dancing at a party. He was tall, with dark hair and sideburns. He had a dimple. He wore a cowboy shirt with red metal buttons. He was a great dancer, the best in the room. I always want to dance with the best dancer and made my way over until we were facing each other. We danced sexy together.

Erik and I had become friends, and Kate agreed he was a good choice. When I was ready, I asked Erik to have brunch with me. I said I had something I wanted to ask him. He didn't ask what.

We sat down at Figaro Café in Hollywood. My palms were clammy. We read the menu. We ordered. Erik's glasses were crooked, like a wacky professor, but one the students would like. We laughed about his glasses. We chatted. Erik was working on a new play. He had met a guy, but it wasn't serious.

Without warning, I said, "Will you be my sperm donor?"

Erik gasped and nodded and with a huge smile said, "Yeah."

I smiled. "Think about it a little bit."

I went home and into Kate's arms. I was so excited I wanted to pass out cigars. We were really on our way to having a baby.

I asked Kate how she envisioned her role. She said, "I want to be the co-mom, but only if we'll be happy together my whole life."

I didn't ask, When will we know? We had been uncertain about our relationship for the past few years, ever since our second anniversary, when I wrote in her card that I wasn't sure we'd be together forever. Kate cried. She said, "Being with you is like building a house on an earthquake fault line."

Even though I don't think Kate was sure either, expressing doubt in a love letter was the stupidest, most insensitive thing I ever did.

I hoped we would figure it out before a baby came. That

night, I was relieved Kate didn't ask me what I wanted. I was still unsure.

"My role is to listen to you and support you in figuring out exactly what you want," she said.

"Thank you," I said. I felt so much love. This was exactly what I wanted.

"Do you want me to research sperm banks?" she said.

"I don't want a sperm bank. You know that. And we have Erik."

"Just in case."

"No," I said. My heart sank, like it did so often when I wanted Kate's support. Sometimes it felt like she wasn't on my team, like when I invited Ellen DeGeneres to be on the Bike Out board of directors and Kate said, "Start small." Or when I sent my first essay to the *Advocate*, the national gay magazine, Kate suggested I send it to a local weekly newspaper instead.

"Why do I always have to agree with you?" Kate said.

"You don't always, but right now I'm the one having the baby. And you just said you would help me figure out what I want."

"We should research all the options," she said.

"If you really want to do research, we need better health insurance."

"Okay, I'll look into it," Kate said. But she never did.

I called my mom and we had a great talk about what the child would call the donor. My mom suggested Bio Dad or Genetic Father. Even before the kid understands what that means, he or she will understand that this man is different from Daddy. I liked this idea.

Kate and I hashed out different scenarios for levels of donor involvement. The truth was, I didn't know. I didn't know what parenting entailed.

So far, I'd been thinking that we would be the only parents. I thought I wanted to know the essence of the man who would be our donor—to know that he was a good guy—without having him around. But when I thought about Erik, maybe I did want him around.

Erik told me he spoke to his mom and friends and wrote in his journal, and at the end of the week we had brunch again. He handed me a letter and said, "I really want to help you."

He wrote: "You're going to be such a wonderful mother. I'm honored and amazed and thrilled that you asked me to help make this possible. Thank you."

Erik had just agreed to be a part of my life for as long as we lived, and he thanked *me*. I felt a knot in my throat. This, I wasn't expecting: to have huge feelings for Erik. Not sexual feelings, but so much love.

We decided to meet once a week for the next several weeks to discuss our baby-making plan. What role would he play in the child's life? What would the child call him? How would his involvement affect Kate? What if I insisted on public school? What if I moved? How would we get his sperm in me? What were his favorite movies?

"I have to ask you something," I said.

"Go ahead." Erik said. I hesitated.

"I'm afraid I'm being homophobic. I'm being gay male phobic."

Before I said anything else, Erik said, "Are you thinking about AIDS?"

"Yeah, I'm sorry."

"Don't be. I'd think you were a fool if you didn't say anything."

"Will you get tested?"

"Of course."

"I'll find out where."

"I've never had an STD. I've never even had anal sex," Erik said.

"No? Why not?"

"I prefer other things."

"I thought gay men loved anal sex."

"Not all gay men," he said.

Erik was the most amazing man alive. He wanted everything I wanted. He was open and easygoing and creative and smart and adorable.

I didn't expect to be nervous about how Erik felt about me, but I was. It was like we had sex on the first date and now I was afraid something would go wrong and we wouldn't still like each other.

Kate, Erik, and I met for dinner at Figaro Café. Kate put her hand out to shake Erik's in that way that embarrassed me, limp and insecure. Kate didn't seem to look Erik in the eye until she had had a few glasses of wine. Then she fired off questions like she was a news reporter. She was a reporter, but she didn't wait for all his answers, she just kept asking questions.

"Do you want children of your own?"

"Someday."

"Have you always wanted to be a dad?"

"Yeah, but you know, it'll be harder—"

"What will you do?"

"Adopt, maybe. Um."

"Do you have siblings?"

"Two brothers and a sister."

"Do they have kids?"

"One brother does."

"Are you close with the kids?"

"Yes, but they live in Phoenix."

"Are you close with your brother?"

"Yeah."

"How often do you see them?"

"Twice a year, maybe."

"Is that hard for you?"

"I wish, well—"

"What role do you want for your family in this child's life?" Kate was wound up. She seemed self-conscious. I wished she didn't care so much what Erik thought. I wished I didn't care so much.

"I don't know," Erik said.

"Do you want your parents involved?"

"My mom said she wants to be involved if you guys want her to be."

"That's a lot of grandmothers," Kate said. That scared her, I could tell.

"What about your dad? Are your parents still married?"

"No. I don't think he'd be that involved."

"How much involvement do you see from your siblings?"

"Hmmm. As much as I give them, I guess. Maybe none. Maybe a little. It depends on our agreement."

"How do you envision your role?" Kate generously refilled our wine glasses. She seemed to be calming down. "Is there anything that scares you about being the donor?"

"Wow," Erik said. "Thanks for asking. I will honor whatever you guys want, but I don't know how I'll feel when a real baby's in the picture. I'm a little afraid of feeling attached."

When Kate went to the bathroom, I wanted to ask Erik if he thought Kate was off-putting. I wondered if he liked her. I wanted to apologize for her, but I didn't. I was loyal to Kate.

"We'll keep talking," Kate said at the end of the meal.

She lifted her glass and we lifted ours. "To having a baby. To life."

After dinner Erik smiled at both of us and gave Kate a big hug. He said, "You guys are gonna be great parents. You have different strengths and I can sense so much love between you. This is really cool."

Then he hugged me. I was surprised and so relieved.

We decided to freeze Erik's sperm so he could make his donations on his own time and I could use them whenever I ovulated. Erik said he would go to the bank 100 times if I wanted him to. He said there's no such thing as too much work; the outcome will be worth it.

I made Erik an appointment at a sperm bank to get tested for HIV, STDs, motility, and sperm count. It cost $175.

## 8 MONTHS BP

Erik was led into a tiny room with one chair, a TV, and a stack of porn magazines. The TV had two channels: one played *I Love Lucy*, the other pornography. No gay porn.

Erik told me he was afraid to touch anything, including the chair, although everything looked very clean. He said it was difficult to get the sperm into the cup. The angle was awkward.

A week later Erik's sperm count results came in. He scored a 2. The average score for the guys they use at the bank is 20. He tested again a week later. His scores were still so low that two doctors told me it would be unlikely to get pregnant with his sperm. I was a lesbian with male fertility problems.

I got into bed with Kate, crushed. "Our pregnancy effort is foiled. How will we ever find another guy like Erik?" I said.

Kate said, "It really hurts me that you're acting like this."

"Like what?"

"Like there are no other options."

"You know I want to know the donor."

"I want this child to be our child, not yours with some guy."

## 7 MONTHS BP

An invitation to Erik's wedding came in the mail. Was this a joke? I called him right away, and he laughed and said he was marrying his best friend so she could get her green card.

He was a two-timer. He wasn't my donor anymore, but I felt like he was cheating on me.

If he was married, he would no longer be gay under the law, which could present legal problems if he was my donor. If he wanted custody of the kid, then he would appear straight and married. And a straight couple might be deemed more suited for parenthood than a lesbian couple. My mother worried that even his mother might want custody and be deemed more suited for parenthood than a lesbian. I didn't think any of this was an issue with Erik, but this is the kind of stuff people told me to look out for.

Maybe his low sperm count was a blessing. I would have felt indebted to him for the rest of my life. I would have felt obligated to go to his weddings.

## 6 MONTHS BP

Kate and I broke up.

This wasn't our first breakup. We had gotten back together six months previously, after being apart for a year. Kate had had it with me then. She was sick of my indecisiveness about our relationship. Kate wanted a wedding and all I could say was, Maybe.

We were lying in bed one Saturday morning. We had started to have sex and then I stopped. I didn't feel close. I wanted to talk. "Why can't we just fuck," Kate said. But I couldn't. I needed to feel connected and hadn't for months. Kate had been depressed and overworked, and she didn't have it in her to talk. Not even to me.

I didn't want to break up. I wanted more of Kate. But Kate thought I was insatiable. She thought whatever she gave was never enough. And maybe she was right. I never quite felt like I got enough of Kate's attention.

And I was afraid of Kate. It wasn't that I didn't trust her or that I feared she would be unfaithful—not at all. I trusted Kate with everything I had, especially after the first breakup, when she moved out, leaving our cat, Coffee Bean. Kate had wanted a cat and picked Coffee Bean out of a little cage in front of the subway station and brought her home. She loved her for years, but Kate knew Bean would be better off with me. Kate is the most gentle, loving, and trustworthy person I know.

It was Kate's mess and eating habits that shook me. I was afraid that if she couldn't take care of herself, she'd never be able to take care of a baby and me.

Kate said, "If you can't love me the way I am, fuck you."

After a year of regret, I begged her back.

I promised to ignore the mess as long as she hired a house-keeping service; to leave her alone after work for a few hours so she could wind down; and to never say another word about what she ate. Kate was my love and home, and I couldn't live without her.

Then, six months before I got pregnant, we were looking for a house to move into together, standing in the kitchen of a perfect two-bedroom bungalow in Santa Monica. We imag-ined living there, just the two of us and then someday living with a baby, maybe two babies. We were talking about where to put our furniture, and I was having trouble breathing.

This anxiety haunted me throughout our relationship. I felt it strongly, spending the night in Kate's apartment after she moved out. Kate seemed oblivious to her mess. From the safety of the middle of the bed, I looked around. In one corner was the recycling spilling out of a bin, next to the bin was a pile of old journals, used tissues overflowing from the garbage can, shriveled-up tea bags that missed the can, the contents of her pockets (pennies and receipts) all over her dresser, a coffee mug with the remains of days-old coffee, laundry but no basket, stacks of magazines, dirty towels, pens, Kate's press pass, dust and fuzz balls. The apartment was a frat house.

Kate's mess made my neck muscles tense. I was antsy in my own home when she came in, braced for the destruction of order. And I had become a neat freak, when I had never been that neat before. I was afraid Kate's messiness meant that she was a mess inside too.

And there was also her eating habits, which scared me even more than her mess. People often describe love as loving the way they feel about themselves when they're with the one they love. I didn't like myself when Kate and I ate together.

Early in our relationship, we went for a hike. Kate wore shorts and her adorable hiking boots, which always looked a little too big on her. A few years before we met, Kate wore her boots for a month straight on an Outward Bound course in the Wyoming wilderness. She'd wear them with jeans around town, and before we started dating I thought Kate was a nature girl, with her fresh, pretty face, blond hair, and those hiking boots. Kate looked like she could sell Ivory soap on TV.

We drove out to the mountains and stopped at a diner on our way. Kate ordered grilled cheese and French fries. I don't remember what I ordered. We hiked hard. The day was glorious with sunrays and blue sky slicing through the trees. Kate's

T-shirt was wet in the pits and between and under her breasts. We counted up how many people we'd ever kissed and laughed about dater's regret, a condition where, as Kate put it, you wake up one day and wonder what you were thinking. We talked about our life dreams. Kate wanted to write for magazines and write children's books and restore an old Victorian house. She said she wanted lots of kids. I thought she was the sexiest woman alive. We stopped a lot along the trail to kiss. "This is the best day," I said. "It's sunny and pretty, like you." I was falling in love.

On our way home, Kate suggested we stop at the diner again. We did. Kate ordered grilled cheese and French fries, and I panicked. This was not how I imagined our lives. When hiking, we'd eat energy food—almond butter sandwiches on whole wheat bread and organic apples or bananas and carrot sticks and fruit-sweetened oatmeal cookies. We'd pack our provisions and carry them on our backs. We'd have a picnic leaning against a tree.

We wouldn't eat at a greasy diner. Never grilled cheese twice in one day.

When Kate ate Fritos in bed at night I was sure that instead of growing old together in that romantic way, we'd grow fat together, in that awful, stereotype of a lesbian way. It would only take time before we were sitting up in bed watching college football, eating Ding Dongs and drinking Pabst Blue Ribbon from cans.

I'd learned enough in women's studies classes in college to know that I was experiencing internalized homophobia. It was one thing to become fat, which I worried about enough to avoid, but becoming a fat lesbian was everything I dreaded. When I felt fat, I felt butch. And I didn't want to be one of the butch lesbians—the ones who are often awkward in their bodies.

I knew the butch lesbians took the brunt of oppression because straight people could spot them on the street. I admired them for refusing to conform to society's standards for women and insisting on being themselves. I realized they paved the way for the rest of us. But they are the lesbians people hate. They are the ones who are accused of being men. And even though I didn't look like them, I always feared I was one piece of cake away.

Maybe all this fear stemmed from my 13-year-old self. When I had to get dressed for Scott Wasserman's bar mitzvah, I didn't feel right in a dress. Around puberty I was thick and clumsy. All through high school I couldn't get dressed without trying on everything in my closet before deciding on the exact same outfit every day—an extra-large T-shirt and jeans.

I was sad and angry that, at 34 years old, I still cared what people thought. I still wanted to fit in. And the irony was, I did. Fifteen years ago, I lost my baby fat and learned to trust my body. I could eat whatever I wanted and stay lean and muscular even though I never lifted weights. I was proud of my arms. I even felt sexy in a dress.

I also loved Kate's body. When we met, she was strong and zaftig, the way I think women look best. But she complained that her boobs were too big and her body was too fat and she rarely felt comfortable in anything except jeans. Like many athletic lesbians I know, Kate hated her breasts. This always broke my heart.

Kate played soccer in high school. Her team was in a big game, and Kate was running downfield. Thinking about Kate running always made me smile: her breasts bouncing gently under her shirt, her cheeks and lips flushed red from exertion, the hair around her forehead darkened with moisture. I always thought she was the most beautiful when she exercised. She looked like she looked having sex.

Kate had possession of the ball when her bra broke. The bra didn't just come unsnapped, but broke beyond repair. I don't know if the fans could tell or if only her teammates knew why she sat on the bench for the rest of the game. I can only imagine her high-school-girl humiliation. Her coach, a middle-aged man, said, "Is there any way you can strap those down?"

I had heard this story several times. When she told me, I thought it meant she was becoming more accepting of her breasts. She knew their effect on me.

"You have the most beautiful breasts in the world," I said.

"They make me so fat. Look at these." Kate cupped them in her hands, lifting one at a time. "They probably weigh twenty pounds each."

"Let me weigh them," I said, putting them in my hands and kissing one and then the other. "You are so beautiful. I love you."

"Oh please, I'm a milch cow." Kate leaned over on top of my face and shimmied her shoulders, slapping my cheeks with her boobs. I laughed hard. She'd do that to me every once in a while. She called it the "car wash."

Kate said, "Would you want my body?"

I thought for a second. "No, but it's perfect on you."

The look on Kate's face told me everything: I was an asshole. I failed her. Why couldn't I have said nothing, or changed the subject? Or I could have so easily and sassily said, "I do want your body." But instead, like an uncensored child or someone with Tourette's Syndrome, I told the truth.

No wonder it didn't matter how many times I said her breasts were beautiful and no matter how much attention I gave them in bed, she still wanted them off. I wanted Kate to know she was beautiful, even though I wouldn't have felt comfortable in her body any more than she did.

During our first few years together, Kate gained 40 pounds.

She carried her weight well and evenly, but the weight gain made me nervous. Was it a reflection of her unhappiness with me? Would it ever stop?

Overeating may have been Kate's issue, but I didn't help. I watched what she ate. I was motivated by love and concern for her health—she knew that—but also by my own fear of getting fat.

"I can't do this," I said.

"What?" She sounded truly surprised.

"I can't live with you."

"What are you saying? When did you start thinking this?"

"I'm sorry," I said. "I'm panicking."

"Why?" Kate started to cry and then I started to cry.

"I'm not happy. We're not happy." I said.

"So, we were never happy before," Kate said. We hugged each other close, laughing a little, but mostly crying, standing on the sidewalk in front of the house in Santa Monica that we never lived in together.

"I love you so much," I said.

We tried everything we could think of for six years to make our relationship work. And I tried, with years of therapy, to separate myself from Kate's problems. But I couldn't. I wanted a co-mom who could emotionally and physically take care of herself and take care of the baby and take care of me. Kate wasn't ready to be a mom, and I couldn't wait anymore.

In the end Kate said, "Fear conquers love."

I told her I wanted her there when the child was born, no matter what happened. I wanted the people I loved to experience this with us, the baby and me: Kate, Stephanie, and my mom.

Erik and I met at Figaro for the last time. Erik was no longer my sperm donor and Kate was no longer my partner. I walked into the restaurant thinking about the time Kate and I sat in the back of Figaro late at night and ordered a glass of wine. We were the only ones in the back, but the waiter seemed to be ignoring us. We finished our wine and wanted another glass. When the waiter came over, Kate said, "Why do you hate us?"

Our waiter smiled really big. He then brought us the rest of the wine bottle, crème brûlée, and a French pastry. "Forgive me," he said. His name was Sébastien, one of the names we'd picked out for a boy, and he was tall and good-looking and French. Kate thought he had a crush on me, but I was sure he had a crush on her. I saw him eyeing her. This was one of the rare times Kate played up her breasts. She wore a push-up bra and a tight, low-cut, black shirt with a wide collar and cleavage. I loved it when men noticed her.

He sat down with us and poured us another glass of wine. He had a glass too. He told us we were beautiful without sounding sleazy. Kate said, "You're beautiful." I nodded. He was.

Kate was mostly shy, but that night she was sassy and disarming, which was a side of her that always seduced me. "You two kiss," she said.

"No you two kiss," I said. Kate turned to Sébastien, and he took her face in his hands and kissed her with his gigantic mouth.

"Oh my god! You can't kiss her like that." I said. "Let her lead." They tried again, but he was terrible.

"Like this," I said and kissed Kate softly, slowly opening my mouth.

Sébastien only charged us for two glasses of wine.

We went home and had one of the sexiest nights we'd ever had together.

Kate and I met in Washington, DC, when she was only 23 and I was 27. I'd see her everywhere, with her reporter's badge hanging on a chain around her neck. She worked for the *Blade*, the largest gay weekly newspaper in the country, and was a celebrity in our lesbian world, covering every story that pertained to us. I thought Kate was very pretty, but I told a friend she was too tomboyish for me. Then one night, I saw her at a bar in a tight tank top and jeans and noticed her womanly body.

Once, I caught Kate standing in the bookstore reading about Susan Smith, the woman who killed her sons by driving her car into a lake. Kate was embarrassed to be reading a book she thought was crappy and sensationalistic and closed it quickly. She slowly admitted her fascination, and I was impressed that she had nearly finished the whole thing. We stood for an hour talking about whether morality is learned or innate and agreed that it's probably both before going to a coffee shop.

We were both unattached and had a Sunday to do with what we pleased. Kate said that it was the first time in history that so many young, single women lived alone. Kate complained that so many choices made it hard to decide what to do with her life. She said she was nostalgic for a world before mass transit, before people lived so far from home. I agreed, but reminded her how hard it would have been to be a lesbian 100 years ago.

"Yeah, but we wouldn't have to deal with annoying housemates," Kate said.

"What do you mean?"

"My housemate wants to bleach the basement and mulch the front lawn."

"How mulch is it?" I asked.

When Kate laughed hard, I thought: I like her. I drank a decaf mocha, and Kate had lemonade and a chocolate-chip cookie, and I was charmed by her. She was brainy and child-like.

We became friends, and Kate invited me to a Jewel concert. The woman she had been dating for a few months was out of town. After the concert, we went back to the big, old house where I lived and danced to the number 10 song on the soundtrack more than 20 times. Kate started it over so many times we learned the lyrics: "Dreams last so long, even after you're gone. I know you love me and soon you will see, you were meant for me and I was meant for you." We danced close and moved really well together.

I told Kate I thought for the first time that sex could be easy and natural. She smiled.

A month later she broke up with the woman she was dating. I said, "I want you to kiss me." The kiss was easy and natural.

It didn't take long to create our dream. We would quit our jobs, have a baby, and spend a year in a villa in the south of Spain. We would steam fresh vegetables for the baby. We would walk through the cobblestone streets, buying olives, taking turns holding the baby in a sling. We would spend the evenings improving our Spanish with the locals in the Plaza Mayor.

I still have the picture Kate gave me, representing our dream: a black-and-white, old-fashioned photo of a chubby, curly-headed baby on roller skates, screaming, crazy with joy. A perfect combination of the two of us. Under the picture Kate hyphenated our names: "Eliot Fox-Askowitz." Eliot was the name of a woman we knew from Spain. We thought it was a perfect name for a boy or a girl.

Erik found me in the corner of the restaurant and sat down. He asked me how I was doing, and I said I missed Kate so much I felt sick. I couldn't focus. I also said I was sad about him. He said he was sad too. He was sorry. I said it wasn't his fault, which he knew was true. I asked him if he felt his manhood was threatened. He didn't. He was just disappointed that he couldn't help me get pregnant.

We hugged and he smelled familiar, like Kate, the way she smelled after a long drive in her Toyota Camry. I told him, and he was surprised. He also drove a Toyota Camry.

Maybe that's why I liked him so much.

## 5 MONTHS BP

My dad called at 8 A.M. He loves to wake me, but this morning I got up at 7. "Do you think a child needs a father?" I asked.

"No," he said. "Doesn't half the world grow up without a father?"

"Probably, but wouldn't it be better for my child to know its father?"

"If you're not going to be with him, we don't need him," he said. "Truth is, a kid needs a mother more than a father."

I called my mom to ask her if she thought a kid needs a father. "Your child will be lucky to have you with or without a father," she said.

"Thanks, Mom. I'm thinking about an anonymous sperm donor."

"I like that idea," she said. She was worried about the legal and emotional complications that could have arisen from a known donor's family. "This is the safest route. This is your baby. My only concern is how do they control how many babies each donor produces? What if our baby falls in love with a half-sibling without even knowing it?"

"They retire a donor's sperm after fifteen offspring or after his sperm runs out," I said.

"Fifteen is a lot," she said.

"Yeah, but it's worldwide and I think the possibility of running into a sibling is extremely small. Also, anyone's dad could have gotten other women pregnant without anyone knowing. For all I know, I have brothers and sisters out there."

The business of picking a sperm donor felt a lot like Internet dating. You browse online through a list of hundreds of donors and get, at first glance, his height, weight, hair color, eye color, and nationality. You also see which donors submitted a baby picture (so you can see the guy's features without his identity being revealed) and which have done an audio interview.

The front page of the Cryobank's online donor catalog read "Click here to view our list of donors with at least one Jewish ancestor." Right away you can narrow your search for Jews. There were no other "click here"s for any other type of person. Amazing, just 60 years ago in Europe, Nazis were trying to de-Jew the world to create a pure Aryan breed; now Jewish genes are the most sought after.

Then, and still for free, you download a two-page list of questions answered in the donor's handwriting: year of birth, educational background, skin tone, math skills, mechanical know-how, artistic and athletic abilities, hobbies, talents, favorite foods, travel interests, description of personality, and where he sees himself in 20 years. From here, you pay $10 for a long profile consisting of his medical history and the history of any diseases or mental disorders in his extended family. Plus $25 for the baby picture and $35 for the audiotape. (Or, with the package deal, you can get the long profile, the baby picture, and the audiotape for $55.)

Lisa said she didn't know half that stuff about my brother before having three kids with him. But still, I worried about the donors' credibility. So I spoke to the vice president of marketing at the Cryobank, who assured me that lying was unlikely. She said sperm donation is a job that requires at least a one-year commitment. The donors are interviewed several times by three different screeners who ultimately get to know them. If the facts, such as college history or SATs or work history, sound unlikely or if his reporting is inconsistent, the screeners double-check. The donors also go through what she called a pedigree, which is an intense interview with a trained genetic counselor to check the plausibility and desirability of his medical history.

The men visit the bank as often as three times a week to make their donations and earn $75 a sample, up to $900 a month. That's $10,800 a year. Not bad. If a man gets creepy or if one of the screeners suspects he's lying, he's fired.

A friend's sister worked at a sperm bank a few years ago. She concurred that it would be very hard for the donors to lie. One of her screening criteria was to imagine using each donor's sperm for herself. If she wouldn't use him, she'd fire him. I felt a lot better having spoken to an insider.

Some banks have their donors sign an agreement to disclose their identity when the offspring turns 18. I thought I wanted to meet my donor someday. I called the Sperm Bank of California in Berkeley, known as a progressive bank, to ask about their donor identification policy.

The woman on the phone was as phony as a car salesman. "Hi. So glad you called," she said, as if she knew me. She said her bank had the most open policy in the country and that most donors agree to be identified. I asked about what happens when the children meet their donors. She said it was a fairly new policy and that not many offspring and donors have met, but that from what she'd heard, all had gone well.

I asked if many women buy several vials of sperm at once.

She got so excited by this idea: "Yes, and right now we're having a special on one of our donors who has been with us for several years. He's Italian and very nice. We could probably sell you twenty vials for the price of ten."

"Why is this guy so cheap?"

"Because we have so much of his sperm in stock. He's a delightful man. Would you like me to send you his profile?"

I said yes, but this was not how I imagined picking my baby's biology—from the sale rack.

When I got his profile, I thought he seemed desirable enough, except he was five foot seven. His father was only five foot two. Too short. I thought this might be why he wasn't selling.

As I contemplated wanting to know the donor, The LA *Times* printed an article about open-identification donors. The first children of open banks were turning 18 and meeting their donors. The article was written from two of the donors' perspectives. Both men were excited but overwhelmed to meet their offspring. The meeting was so emotional for one man that he said he didn't know if he could go through that experience again. But he might have to. He might have sired nine more.

What will happen if my child wants to meet the donor and we're the tenth child he's meeting? Or even the second or third? That wouldn't be very special.

The California Cryobank—probably the biggest bank in the country, located right here in Los Angeles—felt like the one. At the Cryobank, the donor enters into the contract agreeing to stay completely anonymous. They feel that a man shouldn't be asked to make a decision about revealing his identity 18 or more years in advance. If my child and I want to meet our donor when he or she is 18, the bank will facilitate locating him and asking if he's open to a meeting. I trusted that if my child wants to meet the donor, then the donor will want to meet my child.

I wanted a tall Caucasian with dark hair and light eyes, with a picture and an audiotape. I was looking for someone who looked like me. I think this is probably what everyone does, maybe subconsciously, when choosing a mate. Lesbians definitely do it, even if choosing a mate has nothing to do with breeding. I call it Lesbian Narcissism. It goes like this: A lesbian spots another lesbian. She thinks, Oh, she's cute. She notices her clothes. She thinks, Cool outfit. Slowly it dawns on her that she has that same outfit. And the same haircut.

So I was looking for sperm that looked like me. I was careful, though, not to get a full-bred Jew. I knew I was defying the logic of my people because, like most Jewish girls, I grew up hearing "You'll marry a nice Jewish boy." The theory goes that Jewish boys are smart, hardworking, good providers who stray less than other boys. I don't doubt the theory, but I wasn't looking for a provider and I had done some reading and found that Jews carry certain diseases at a higher rate than the general population. Many racial and ethnic groups, especially those that encourage marrying within the group, carry genetic disorders that thereby occur more frequently within those groups. Scary.

Because Jews before me have been just as paranoid as I am and have invested money in studying disease trends in our people, I know that Jews carry Tay-Sachs, Gaucher disease, Canavan disease, Niemann-Pick disease, Bloom syndrome, Crohn's disease, and more. These diseases give us irritable bowels, broken bones, collapsed central nervous systems, and with some of the more serious diseases, a five-year life expectancy. So in my attempt to create the strongest, healthiest, most vital and superior offspring, and since I'm 100 percent Jewish, I wanted a mutt.

With these stipulations, I narrowed the field from hundreds to 20.

Stephanie and I sat down to review the short profiles I'd chosen. Steph is a sharp reader and a fast shopper. She was quick to cut candidates. A spelling or grammatical error, and he was out. If he sounded too pretentious, he was out. I appreciated her decisiveness. I trusted her. And this was too big to do alone. In less than an hour we were down to three.

Donor number 1444 was a top contender. He was from Belarus, and it was clear English was not his first language. Under Hobbies, he wrote: "I like the nature." Stephanie tried to nix him. "Russia's out," she said. "What will you tell your kid: He likes the nature?"

"I like the nature," I said.

Donor 5599 got 1550 on his SATs. "5599 looks good," I said. Smart sperm, that's what I wanted.

"Okay, there's nothing offensive about his answers," Steph said.

Donor 3342 didn't write with the neatest handwriting, but he passed for grammar and spelling. He likes Indian food, sushi, and Tex-Mex. He's a writer. He wrote that his artistic talent consists of decorating his apartment. Math is not his favorite subject. He's not mechanically inclined, but hopes to someday learn to fix his car. He's funny. Stephanie said he's her favorite.

I paid $165, the package deal for my top three candidates, and got their long profiles, audiotapes, and baby pictures.

5599's brother was diagnosed and treated for obsessive-compulsive disorder at 21. He wrote: "My brother's health is excellent. He's taking medication, and he's fine now." His maternal grandmother drank herself to death at 45. He'd probably say she's fine now. He was out.

Russia came from a healthy family. And he was an adorable baby. But when he was asked in his audio interview why he wanted to donate sperm, he said, "I want to very badly to help some one who is less fortunate." No. Too serious.

3342 is allergic to cats and is nearsighted, but that seemed like the worst of it. When I saw his baby picture and heard his voice on tape, I knew he would be mine. In his picture he's about 3 years old, with shaggy, dark hair and pouting lips. He's wearing overalls. 3342 said, "I thought donating sperm would be a fun way to make some extra cash."

### 4 MONTHS BP

Bike Out was having a cash-flow crisis. The Bush administration drastically reduced state funds for social services, so big local agencies were relying on private foundations. Small organizations, like ours, were being squeezed out of the funding pool. We needed individuals to step up or we'd go under.

Kids relied on us. We were one of very few places anywhere that gay and lesbian young people felt safe. I sent an e-mail to the 500 youth in our database telling them we needed help. The next Saturday, Ariel and Michael took the Metro and a bus, an hour and a half each way, from Long Beach to our office in Santa Monica to help fix bikes for our next bike sale. Selling used bikes was one of our best fund-raisers.

I met Ariel, two years before, when she was 15, during orientation for our weeklong expedition. Her given name was José (she was born a boy), but she preferred being a girl and being called Ariel away from home. Her mother didn't know. At that meeting she looked like a very slight Latino boy, with cherry-red lips and bright green eyes. I've since seen her become a beautiful woman.

I told the group of boys and girls what to bring and what to expect for our trip: "There will be no cell phones, no pagers, no radios, no deodorant, and no makeup."

"I can't go without my lipstick and glitter, girl!" Ariel said. By the third day of the trip, everyone was wearing glitter.

Michael was 17 and barely hanging on in school, but he was one of the smartest kids I knew. When a conflict came up on his first expedition and most of the others wanted to avoid the tension, Michael told the entire group that resolving the conflict would make everyone closer. Michael's father was a drug addict and his mother, just 33, had four children to take care of alone. His parents didn't know he wanted to be a dancer. He told me no one had ever believed in him like we did. He wanted to do whatever he could to keep Bike Out alive.

I loved these kids. And without Bike Out, what would I have? Where would I show up every day?

I called all past donors and everyone I knew to beg for money. Courting donors had been my job for the last five years. I knew I was good at it; the biggest trick was simply to ask, but asking and asking took its toll. I always had to be polite.

What a relief it would be to have an anonymous donor.

I called my dad, who's not poor, and asked him for $1,000. He said, "I don't know." Then he gave me some line about only calling him for money, which was entirely false, and how he'd given me money my whole life.

"Dad, I'm not trying to buy a new outfit," I said. "I'm trying to help some kids stay away from drugs and prostitution."

Later that day he called me back. He said, "I thought about it. I realize if you can't ask your family for donations, who can you ask?" He sent $1,000.

I called my mom and asked her for $1,000. My parents had been separated for five years, so I could sort of double-dip.

She's a professional quilter and real estate owner. She could afford it. My mom said yes, no problem. She was always my easiest and most generous donor.

I bought ten vials of donor 3342 because on average it takes six months for a 35-year-old woman to get pregnant, and that's when she's having sex with a man. Since frozen sperm may not work as well, I got ten tries, so I could relax without worrying about running out. If I got pregnant right away, and if the kid came out pretty good, I'd have sperm left over for another one. Or maybe someday I'd get myself a young wife who'd have a baby, and then our children would have the same genetic father. Someday I might be a mom and a dad.

One sample cost $250. The bank charged an additional $40 to get each sperm vial out of the bank, or $70 for same-day pickup. So the actual cost was $250 for sperm plus $70 for pickup, or $320 a freeze pop.

Artificial inseminations are handled at Kaiser's Infertility Clinic for $36. At my first appointment, I told the nurse, a broad black woman with a warm face, I wished they'd change the name. "Fertility Clinic would be a lot more positive," I said. She agreed. She said that I would be assigned a new doctor, a fertility specialist, who would assess what was wrong with me.

She patted my butt to lead me down the hall and said, "We're going to get you pregnant." I wanted to hug her. She sat me down alone in a small room and had me watch a mandatory video, "Infertility: The New Solutions." The video featured three heterosexual couples with various fertility problems. One couple just wasn't having enough sex.

I learned that if you have sex less than once a week you have a 17 percent chance of getting pregnant within six months. Sex once a week almost doubles your chances to 32 percent. Twice a week and you have a 46 percent chance, and three times a week gives you a 51 percent chance of getting pregnant within six months.

When the video was over, I told the nurse I'd discovered my problem.

"What is it?"

"I'm a lesbian."

She seemed too dignified to smile, but made a face that told me she'd seen it all.

The doctor was an adorable old man, who reminded me of my uncle Murray: bald and smart and kind and trustworthy. He told me about my medical options: "There are several very effective drugs we can use. I recommend starting with Clomid, which will tell us exactly when you ovulate."

"Shouldn't I try first without drugs?"

"It depends how long you want to wait. You're approaching thirty-five, but of course, it's up to you." I always get the feeling, with my uncle Murray, that he loves me and supports my endeavors but thinks I'm a little bit naive, maybe in a way that he admires, but I'm not always sure. I got the same feeling with my doctor, like he was thinking, How sweet; she wants to try without meds. He pulled out a sheet of paper charting the probability of getting pregnant at different ages. According to his chart, I should have started 15 years ago.

I tried to get pregnant, the first time, a week before flying to New York for the unveiling of Robin's tombstone, one year after she died. I was sure I was pregnant. I had been eating Thai food and Fudgesicles all week. I thought that was a sign. I told Stephanie I felt something in my womb. Not pain, but more like activity from the inside.

She said, "Hmmm, I don't think so."

I said, "I do, I feel the cells dividing."

"You can't feel anything."

"And my boobs are bigger and they hurt."

"Yeah," she said. "That's what you feel when you're pre-menstrual."

Janet had also tried, and neither of us knew yet, for sure, if we were pregnant. When anyone asked how I was doing, I said, "I might be pregnant." Janet said nothing. She was cool that way.

About a hundred friends and family members were gathered at the cemetery, surrounding the spot where we buried Robin. Seeing a headstone with her name on it made me queasy, like looking at a gory accident. I stared, but I didn't want to see. Robin Weinstein Ross, mother, sister, daughter, niece, soul mate... *Soul mate* was repeated a million times last year at the funeral. And here it was, engraved into her tombstone forever. Even if it was true, Robin was not sentimental or effusive. I couldn't help thinking this would have embarrassed her.

Gregory said he was lucky to have spent the last 15 years with an angel. (A year ago, standing out in the cold like we did that day, Gregory said 14 years.) Gregory was not bitter. He said he missed Robin's physical presence, but felt her with him every moment, deep in his soul. He didn't worry about the future and he didn't rush any of the 525,600 minutes of the past year, even if the moment he was in was unbearable. He was referring to a song from the musical *Rent* that he sings with his 4-year-old.

If Gregory can accept the loss of Robin, and even find meaning and beauty in it somehow, then maybe I can accept the end of my relationship with Kate. Thank God Kate's alive.

After the ceremony, we went to Robin's house, where, in typical Jewish fashion, the women in Robin's life had set up a buffet. It was so strange to be eating tuna fish on a bagel in her house without her. Robin and I must have eaten tuna on a bagel 100 times at Phil's Deli, where we'd stop on our way to the beach when we were skipping school.

Janet and I stuck close to each other for the rest of the day. We didn't want to be apart for a second. We even went to the bathroom together.

As soon as I was back home in Los Angeles, Janet called. She was pregnant. I was the first person she told, after her husband.

I got off the phone and peed on a pregnancy test stick. Only one pink line. I called Janet back and said, "I set myself up for disappointment."

She said, "You were just having fun with the idea of being pregnant."

"What if I'm infertile?"

"You're not."

"You don't know."

"I know."

It's possible to get a false negative, so I tested two more times that day and the next. Four tests were negative. Then I got my period.

## 3 MONTHS BP

In the days leading to ovulation, I was ready to pounce. I had a drink with a friend at a lesbian bar, the Normandie Room. The owner, Michael, the only man in the place, knew my friend and sat down with us. My insides got hollow. I felt a stirring between my legs. I told him he was the hottest girl in the bar. He laughed. He told me he was married, but I kept flirting. I asked if he would host a fund-raiser for Bike Out, and he said yes.

We met again, a week later, to discuss the Bike Out fund-raiser. When he walked into the restaurant, where I was already seated at a table for two, I did a double take. I wanted to rub my eyes with my fists like they do in cartoons. Michael looked so small. Puny. He had pretty eyes, but in the light his skin looked pocked and his hair was receding fast. He was okay, but no stud.

I must have been really drunk the night we met. We had a cordial business meeting and then I went home to check my ovulation chart. I met Michael at the Normandie Room the night before my temperature spiked. I was in heat.

When my body was preparing for the possibility of getting pregnant, I felt a huge loss. I had no one to have sex with. I was bypassing sex, bypassing the vagina entirely, and inserting the sperm right into my uterus, cutting out five hours of travel time for my sperm. I learned recently that cervixes suck and pull like a vacuum cleaner during an orgasm to facilitate the movement of the sperm toward the egg. For a second I thought I should have the doctor leave me alone after insemination. But no need; the sperm was going straight into my uterus.

I wanted love.

## 2 MONTHS BP

The ovulation test sticks were useless, and they were all I had. I needed two equally dark lines so I would know when my luteinizing hormone was triggering ovulation. The LH surges 24 to 36 hours before the egg is released from the ovary, which is ample time to get sperm inside the vagina, no matter what method you choose. Fresh sperm can live inside a woman for up to seven days, but with frozen sperm, no one knows. Some theories say frozen sperm lasts only 12 hours.

Janet didn't get two equally dark lines but got pregnant anyway. I didn't have the luxury of trying without a positive stick.

Here's what I had to deal with: On day 22 of my cycle, I

was trying to live my normal lesbian life and was spending the night in the Santa Monica Mountains with a group of women I call the Lesbian Campers. I didn't know most of them well, except Andrea Stern.

Kate and I had gone Lesbian Camping twice with this group. The first time, everyone gathered around a picnic table and played Celebrity, a game where each side picks famous names out of a hat and tries to describe the names to their teammates. In the first round, you can use words. In the second round, you can use only one word; the third round is like Charades. Kate was so adorable playing; jumping around with her finger sticking out in front of her crotch. The finger had become the universal sign for man. She was dancing wildly, pretending to play the guitar, acting out Jimmy Hendrix. I couldn't wait for the game to end so I could take Kate back to our tent.

The last time we went Lesbian Camping together was a few weeks before we finally broke up. Kate wasn't up for a weekend with other people, but she didn't know that until we were already there. The first day, Kate read the newspaper for eight hours straight and barely spoke to anyone, including me. For most of the day, the group gathered in a loose circle, sitting on collapsible camping chairs. We made breakfast and then lunch. Some people went on a hike or played Frisbee. Kate read her newspaper.

Someone passed around a joint, and I got stoned and very paranoid. "I'm not having fun," I said. Kate looked up from her paper but didn't say anything. Maybe I was anxious because Kate and I were having trouble. Maybe I was anxious because Kate was being antisocial.

Andrea Stern pulled her chair between Kate and me. She said, "You need to talk." I did. Kate looked pissed. I felt like she was judging me for being stoned or for trying to get attention. I was judging her, for sure.

This time, I went Lesbian Camping alone. I woke up and right away took my temperature—98.2 degrees, on the low side, which meant the LH hadn't surged and I hadn't yet ovulated.

A woman ovulates 14 days *before* her next period, but knowing in advance when that day will be is hard to predict, especially with an inconsistent cycle. For the last two years, I'd taken my temperature at the same time every morning to chart the day my temperature spiked—the day after ovulation. I charted for morale mostly. To psych myself up.

The length of my cycle varied from 30 to 45 days, and some cycles came and went without a rise in temperature, which meant no egg was released. Somewhere between days 15 and 30, I would notice vaginal mucus, the secretions that resemble egg whites, which provide a slick ride for sperm. Vaginal mucus means ovulation is coming. Usually, on one of the days after noticing vaginal mucus, my temperature would be close to 99 degrees, indicating that I had ovulated the day before.

There was a lot to remember: slippery secretions happen before ovulation, basal body temperature spikes after ovulation, LH surges before ovulation. Before trying to get pregnant I didn't think about the days of my menstrual cycle or ovulation or my vaginal mucus. Suddenly, I was bogged down in math and science.

I crawled out of my tent. It had been a cold night, and camping alone exaggerated the cold. Even though Kate wasn't always easy to be around, I missed her. She was my warm teddy bear.

Instead of going to the bathroom, I headed for the trees. I walked past the picnic tables where women were already making coffee and breakfast. Andrea Stern was chopping vegetables for an omelet. I waved my ovulation stick at Andrea and she gave me a nod.

I peed in the woods on my stick and fantasized about getting two dark purple lines. I knew I should be ovulating any
day, because when I wiped after peeing my vagina felt like a
Slip-n-Slide, and since there's only one other explanation for
such slickness and since I couldn't remember the last time I
had sex, I knew ovulation was pending. But the test line that
morning on the camping trip was lighter than the control
line—negative—like it had been for days. Same negative stick
like my last cycle and the cycle before that and the cycle before that and before that. I walked back to the picnic tables.
"Nothing," I said to Andrea.

She said, "Let it go. God is your driver." I laughed ner-
vously, the way I laughed in elementary school when I knew
I was getting in trouble. I tried not to, but I couldn't help
laughing whenever Andrea got religious on me. She knew it
made me nervous, but she'd do it anyway.

I don't know why the mention of God made me laugh.
Maybe because it scared me that Andrea was a believer. I
always thought people who believed in God might not be so
smart. But Andrea was, and I admired her conviction. Maybe
it made me nervous because I wasn't sure what I believed. I
said: "Oh, I've seen that bumper sticker. I thought it said Dog
is your driver." She lowered her eyebrows.

## 1 MONTH BP

I needed a better ovulation testing system, so I bought a
Clear Plan Easy Fertility Monitor with a built-in computer
for $225.

I had the money. With the help of my parents, I had made
some good real estate investments, so I felt prepared, finan-
cially at least, to raise a child. Still, $225 for an ovulation test
kit made me feel desperate, or like I'd been had.

I went to my therapist and told her I thought I might be
feeling a little stressed. I said that I'd heard stress was bad for

ovulation and that maybe I was stressing myself out so badly trying to time everything right that I didn't ovulate at all.

She said, "Of course. What you're attempting to do is very brave, especially alone."

"I know, but millions of women have babies alone," I said.

"Let yourself see the difficulty in this. It's okay to be afraid."

We had spent many sessions talking about my fear of being afraid or sad. How I have trouble accepting my vulnerability. Right then I thought she was probably right. I was afraid to be afraid.

## 1 Day BP

I woke up at 8 A.M., and even though the directions for the Fertility Monitor said first morning urine is not the best, I peed on a stick. I had to pee anyway. And just in case my LH had surged in the last eight hours, while I'd been sleeping, I didn't want to miss it.

The monitor said Low Fertility.

I decided to follow the instructions to the letter. I wouldn't drink water, and I wouldn't pee for at least two hours, then I'd test again.

My therapist suggested I plant seeds to symbolize the growth of seeds in my womb.

With a huge shovel, I tilled the earth. I dug hard for hours. I loosened the soil, added mulch, and planted seeds: lavender, mint, sage, and a little cat grass for Coffee Bean.

At 3:30 in the afternoon, my fertility monitor said Peak Fertility. I ran outside and checked my garden. I ran back in. I looked at the monitor again. Peak Fertility! I jumped up and down, shaking out my arms and legs like I was about to run the 100-meter dash. Then I called the clinic and made an appointment for 12:30 the next day. If my calculations were correct, I'd be inseminating three hours before the first chance of ovulation. I feared this was too early. I didn't want my sperm tiring themselves out before getting to the egg. The worst mistake is inseminating too late.

## CONCEPTION

After 45 minutes in the lobby of the Kaiser Infertility Clinic, I was led into a private, well-lit room. A very nice nurse-practitioner—the Inseminator, I called her—had me change into a hospital gown, lie back on the table, and put my feet in the metal stirrups. The room was a typical, cheerful gynecological exam room except for the AIDS poster pinned to the bulletin board next to the bed. The caption read "A Deadly Saturday Night Special." The picture showed two man/woman couples, one black and one Latino, with a skeleton lurking behind them. The other posters—The Female Reproductive System and Learning About Your Breasts—were benign enough. Cheap-looking pamphlets about STDs, fibroids, and menopause hung in a rack nailed to the wall by the door. There was also a scale, a white cabinet with medical tools, and a sink. The room smelled like soap.

The Inseminator and I chatted about her daughter, who she hoped would someday have a baby. I told her I was doing this alone. She said she was impressed, and wondered if her daughter might also have a baby alone because she's very overweight. The Inseminator thinks fat people and lesbians have babies alone.

She inserted a speculum, like I was getting a Pap smear, and with a very thin 15-inch-long strawlike device connected to a syringe, directed the sperm through my vagina, through my cervix, and into my uterus. That was it. Without any pain, in less than 30 seconds, I was inseminated. Then I went back to work.

On this particular day, Bike Out was having a bike sale and the office was busy. Even after my last letdown, I told everyone I knew that I had just gotten inseminated.

# Second Trimester

I have graduated into the second trimester. Why don't I feel better?

Today I go to yoga, a class specifically designed for pregnant women, because, as every day, I need to relax. Just the thought of committing to an hour-and-a-half class without food makes me queasy. But I'm a mother who tries to do right by her kid.

At only four weeks, when I was not yet showing and just beginning to feel nauseated, I tried yoga. The teacher asked, "Does anyone have any injuries I should know about. Is anyone pregnant?" I couldn't raise my hand. There were about 30 people in the class and I didn't want them to look at me. I had never before cared who looked at me. I normally like it when people look at me. But in that yoga class, I was like one of those college girls in a lecture who knows the answer but doesn't put her hand up all the way. My heart was pounding. When the teacher walked by me to adjust a student, I whispered that I was pregnant. She told me not to do any twisting poses. I hardly did *any* poses for fear of losing my baby. I thought maybe I was having a heart attack.

Today the class is taught in a tiny room with just four students—all of us pregnant. The first few minutes seem promising. Then, as we stand with our legs spread wide apart and our heads dangling toward the floor, the teacher instructs us to open our mouths wide and exhale fully. "Roar," she says. "This is called 'Lion's Breath.'"

Now, I'm no dentist, but my uncle is, and I can say with certainty that this prenatal yoga teacher has gum disease. Every time she demonstrates Lion's Breath, my eyes water and I gag and fight to suppress vomiting. This teacher is fond of Lion's Breath.

I quit yoga.

## WEEK 13, DAY 4
Janet calls me weeks after sending me the ugly skirt. She says, "It's polite to thank a person when she gets you a present."

"Jan," I say. "Who were you shopping for?"

## WEEK 13, DAY 5
Ravi and Stephanie are here cleaning my house. Steph is worried about me. Ravi gives me a lecture. "The outside reflects the inside, blah, blah."

I say, "No shit. I'm depressed."

## WEEK 14
My dad calls. He asks how I'm doing, and I say, "I've gained 14 pounds. I feel like a stuck pig."

"Go easy on the ice cream," he says.

"Don't tell me what to eat. I have to go." Fuck him. Like I'm having fun here at the all-you-can-eat buffet. Men are such idiots. They have no understanding of weight and a woman's body.

My mom calls to ask if I want a quilt. "Yeah!" I say. "What are you thinking?"

"I've been wanting to depict Demeter and Persephone."

"Who?"

"In Greek mythology, Demeter is Persephone's mom, the goddess of the harvest." It's the myth that explains the seasons."

"That's for me?"

She says it's about us: about growing up and a mother's struggle to let go. She tells me that Persephone was abducted by Hades, the god of the underworld, and Demeter missed her so much she froze the earth. When Persephone came back, Demeter thawed the earth again.

Persephone would have been free forever except she made a deal with Hades that if she ate in the underworld she'd have to go back. She ate some pomegranate seeds, some say, in an act of love. Now, every year, Persephone goes to the underworld for a few months, and while she's gone, her mother makes the earth freeze.

"You wouldn't see us this way if you didn't think I went to hell."

WEEK 14, DAY 3
I have to be careful brushing and flossing. Anything in my mouth makes me want to hurl.

WEEK 14, DAY 4
I'm on a mission to find the man behind 3342. I think I see

him everywhere. The man at the next table at Hurry Curry has dark wavy hair and piercing green eyes. 3342 has dark wavy hair and green eyes. 3342 likes Indian food. This guy looks about 29. 3342 is 29. He's beautiful. I think he's my donor.

Stephanie is telling me about problems she's having with her boyfriend, a conversation we've been having a lot lately, but I'm not listening. I am listening to my possible sperm donor talk to a white woman with light-brown dreadlocks. He is saying something about his rising sign and why he and his ex-girlfriend didn't work out.

Sperm Donor says: "I don't know, man. I mean, I'm a Libra and she's an Aquarius. Match made in heaven."

Dreadlocks says, "Do you know her Chinese horoscope, because if she's a dragon, that just makes the whole thing way more volatile."

"I can't get into the whole Chinese horoscope thing," Sperm Donor says. "It just doesn't resonate with me on a soul level."

"I hear you," Dreadlocks says.

Oh no. What if things resonate with 3342 on a soul level?

"In the beginning everything seemed so perfect. It's because her Jupiter and my moon created this massive illusion," he says. This can't be my sperm donor.

"Dude, that sucks."

"Worst part is I waited till things fell apart before looking at her chart. We have five T-squares together. Five!"

"Dude, run. Don't walk."

There is nothing less attractive than someone who believes in the zodiac. This couldn't possibly be my donor. Please don't let this be my donor.

WEEK 14, DAY 5

I'm at a party, which is a mistake. I have no business going to a party where svelte, single people are drinking mojitos and dancing to top hits of the '80s. I feel my clothes shrinking up on me. I feel like Aunt Rose, the name Janet calls me when she catches me turning the music down or heading to bed at nine o'clock. She means I'm a total bore. I should be in my rocker on the porch drinking lemonade without the rum.

But there he is. This man is tall, with dark hair and light eyes. A great dancer. I'm inspired to dance with him. I put down my water and catch his eye while I move to the center of the dance floor. I try to dance exactly like he's dancing: little hip jiggles, shoulders, pursed lips. We're dancing to Marvin Gaye: "I believe in miracles. You sexy thing. You sexy thing, you."

He doesn't notice my belly, or maybe he does. It doesn't matter. I think he's the one.

I lean in and he bends down. "How tall are you?" I ask.

"Six-three"

My donor's 6'2". I have to go home.

WEEK 14, DAY 6

I tell Stephanie I've lost my mind. I say, "I don't know why I'm doing this."

She says, "Why are you doing this?"

I can't stand Stephanie. I vow never to turn a question around on a person who's just said she's lost her mind.

My dad thinks friends don't matter once you get older. Maybe friends don't matter once you have a family. Or maybe friends don't matter even before that, like once you get pregnant. I hate admitting my dad is right about anything.

Now I understand the role of marriage: to lock in the husband. Because when a woman is pregnant, if she's anything like me, she's done. That's it. Not interested. In anything. Certainly not a husband, which explains why so many men have affairs when their wives are pregnant. I don't condone cheating, but I understand now that these men aren't getting any attention. They're certainly not getting any sex.

My attraction is gone. I'm the opposite of attracted. I'm repelled. I'm sure I'm also repellent.

I wonder if lesbians stray when their girlfriends are about to have a baby. Probably. Why not? Why would lesbians be any different? Luckily I don't have a girlfriend.

## WEEK 15, DAY 2

I have an 11 A.M. appointment for amniocentesis. This is the definitive test for spina bifida, Down syndrome, and other chromosomal disorders. For someone 35, doctors recommend amnio. There is a 1 in 134 chance that the kid will have a chromosomal disorder, including Down syndrome, and a 1 in 200 chance the test will cause a miscarriage. Since the probability of having a kid with Down syndrome is higher than the probability of having a miscarriage, I decided to take the test. Also, because when Stephanie and I were discussing whether or not I should get the amnio, she said, "One in a hundred and thirty-four is very unlikely. Way less likely than drawing the ace of spades out of a deck of cards." She grabbed a deck of cards, fanned them out, and said, "Draw."

I drew the ace of spades.

I am not proud of taking the test, but I don't think I could handle a child with Down syndrome alone.

I remember a conversation I witnessed between Janet and her husband when she was pregnant with their first child. Janet was leaning toward taking the test. Her husband said they would love the child no matter what. They would handle it together.

Andrea Stern was supposed to take me to my appointment. I asked her a week in advance. I said I was very nervous and that I wasn't supposed to drive after the test. She said of course she'd take me. Andrea forgot my appointment.

I told Leah, the woman who wears Tom's of Maine deodorant and works in the next office, that I was going alone, and she said, "Absolutely not." She has two children and has had two amnios.

She shows up with a bouquet of flowers. This morning I think rotten carrots don't smell so bad.

The doctor looks at the baby through the ultrasound. I can make out the head this time and maybe the body, but it still looks like a space creature. He says, "I think I got a good look. Do you want to know if it's a boy or a girl?"

I say, "No, but a good look at what? It's gotta be a boy."

He doesn't say anything else. He sticks a five-inch needle straight into my womb an inch and a half below my belly button and draws out yellow liquid into two large vials, similar to the ones they use for blood, but bigger. I feel it, but it doesn't hurt. Leah told me to talk to my baby during the procedure. "Stay away from the needle, my baby," I say over and over. I'm surprised when tears quietly stream down my face.

The doctor takes 10 percent of my amniotic fluid. The whole procedure is over in five minutes.

## WEEK 15, DAY 4

Two days since amnio and I have barely moved from the couch. Every time I go to the bathroom, I expect to see blood all over my underwear—a miscarriage. I'm surprised when there's nothing. They told me to watch for leaking. I don't quite know what leaking would look like, but as far as I can tell, no leaking.

The doctor said an infection was the most likely cause of

miscarriage, and if one occurred it would occur within five days. He sterilized the operating theater, as they call the area where surgery is performed, but there is still a chance of introducing bacteria into the body. In his 17 years of performing amniocentesis, he admitted that miscarriage had happened about ten times. Just three more days to worry.

Kate comes over to make dinner tonight. I'm not supposed to move much, so this is, for her, a huge gesture in taking care of me. This is also the second time in six years that Kate has cooked our dinner.

She bought wild, river-swimming salmon at the Santa Monica Fish Market for $14.99 a pound, because I am nervous about poisoning my fetus with dyes and antibiotics that are pumped into farmed salmon. She has potatoes and spinach on the stove and the salmon outside on the barbecue. The potatoes are safely in the water, but the salmon needs supervision and the spinach may have been started too early. She flits in and out of the house several times before the salmon gets slightly charred. The garlic never makes it into the spinach, but I'm not in the mood for garlic anyway. Cooking is hard for Kate, and I appreciate the effort. The food is delicious.

The one other dinner Kate cooked for us was eggs sunny-side up over a round scoop of white rice covered with salsa. She called this meal "Bloody Eyeball."

WEEK 16, DAY 2
It's safe to get up from the couch now. My fetus survived amnio. I just have to wait for the results.

Janet is seven months pregnant, works full time, and has a 3-year-old. I don't know how she can manage it. Obviously she's having a blissful pregnancy. Now she and my sister-in-law are throwing me a baby shower, even thought I don't want it, and even though some Jews think a shower before the baby's born is bad luck.

She tells me I have to register for shower gifts at Babies "R" Us. If I have to register somewhere, I want to register at an outdoor store and get a new tent. Janet says, "Forget about it. You're never going camping again."

"Then let people get me whatever they want. Registering is too greedy."

"Andrea, don't miss the opportunity to get the stuff you'll need."

Today I go to Babies "R" Us to pick out the big items like a stroller, car seat, and high chair. I walk in and immediately think of everything I hate about America: It's bright and huge and ugly and plastic. It's overindulgent. It has no soul. There are more than 30 infant car seats to choose from and another 30 for toddlers. Who needs so many choices? I'm in the store fewer than ten minutes, and I start to sweat in the pits. My heart is racing and I think I feel pain in my left shoulder, which is what my grandmother felt the day she dropped dead from a heart attack. I call Janet from my cell phone: "I'm at Babies "R" Us and I can't do it. I think I may have swallowed poison."

"Go home," she says. "I'll pick out what you need."

Janet e-mails me her registry list, including recommendations from Robin, who helped her when Janet first got pregnant. Robin did *Consumer Reports* research. On matters like these, Robin was the final authority. I call Jan to thank her, and she walks me through the Babies "R" Us online registry. It takes more than an hour. She has me pick patterns and colors, but all the items have been decided.

WEEK 16, DAY 4

I am looking at myself naked in a full-length mirror. My nipples have grown longer. My areolas are as wide as silver dollars and dark brown. My breasts are taking the shape of baby bottles.

Lisa calls to tell me I forgot to invite Monica to my baby shower. Monica is the daughter of the woman my dad is going to marry the day before my shower. The woman my dad is going to marry is the woman he cheated with before he left my mom. We know this because my brother and the woman my dad is about to marry worked in the same office. The news of the two of them was like junior high school gossip.

The woman's nice enough, but she represents what happened, so I hate her. Her daughter's actually kind of cool, but I have no interest in liking either of them. Lisa tells me my dad called *her* to ask why Monica didn't get an invitation. Lisa told my dad I must have mistakenly left her off the list.

"No, Lisa, it wasn't a mistake," I say. "I'm not inviting Monica to my baby shower." I'm pissed, but not at Lisa. I'm pissed at my dad. "He knows I would never invite her."

Lisa is upset. She doesn't like conflict and especially doesn't like being in the middle of it. I tell her I'll handle it. I call my dad. I leave messages on his work and cell phones. "I am not inviting Monica to my baby shower," I say.

### WEEK 16, DAY 5

My dad waits a day to call me back. He says, "I am so mad I couldn't even talk to you yesterday." I get a little thrill, like a tingle up my spine, hearing my dad is mad. Nothing ever seems to affect him. This is big. My dad is mad. "Why aren't you inviting Monica?"

"Because she's not my friend and she's not my family."

"She's going to be your family."

"No. She's going to be *your* family."

"I am your father. You have to accept reality. She is part of your family."

"Why should I accept that you cheated on my mother? If your dad cheated on your mother, you wouldn't be so quick to accept."

"Andrea, your mother and I have not been together for five years."

"I'm not saying get back with Mom. I'm saying I don't like what you did, and I don't have to embrace it by inviting your floozy bitch's whole family to my baby shower."

"Do not speak that way about Elsa. What has she done to you?"

"Colluded in cheating on Mom."

"I am so surprised at you. Things happen in life, Andrea."

"Oh, please."

"You're going to be really sorry for what you're doing. You have to grow up sometime."

"No, I don't."

## WEEK 17, DAY 2

My amnio results should be in. I wait all morning for a call from my doctor. I am so distracted I can barely lead the staff meeting at work. I am the boss here at this organization that I nurtured to life. Now I have no interest in it. I ask my staff how their work is going, but I don't pay attention to their answers. I end the staff meeting early so I can call for the results.

An actual person answers the phone, which is a miracle at Kaiser. I say, "I'm calling for my amnio results."

A woman asks me my name, steps away from the phone, and suddenly I feel like I have diarrhea. I don't know if I can hold on much longer. What is she doing?

She returns and says, "You ready?"

"Yeah," I say tentatively.

She says, "Do you want to know if it's a boy or a girl?"

"I'm dying to know, but don't tell me," I say.

She giggles. Now I'm thinking if there was a problem she probably would have mentioned it right away. I hear other people talking in the doctor's office. Why isn't she saying anything? Someone I don't know has come into our office.

"Well, everything looks fine," she says.

"No spina bifida or Down syndrome?"

"No."

I hang up the phone and hug my workmates.

### WEEK 17, DAY 3

I discover swimming. Besides eating, swimming is my only relief. In the water, I feel normal. I can forget I'm pregnant. I am an athlete again.

My arms are strong and my stroke, world-class. I feel it. My form is exactly like Greg Louganis, or is he the diver? I think the lifeguard is going to tap me on the head and invite me to join the YMCA swim team. I'll have to say, "I better not, I'm pregnant."

In the locker room, after my swim, I look at myself in a full-length mirror. Except for the hot-pink bikini, I am staring at my mother: her hips, her thighs, her soft knees.

In the shower I take off my bikini and wash my hair. Three girls, probably 8 years old, come in, giggling. They keep their suits on while they shower. I see them eyeing me sideways, catching glimpses of me naked and full-bodied. I can't believe I have become one of those ladies in the locker room.

### WEEK 18

I go to a single mom's support group. I figure I need support.

Fifteen women and their children are sitting around a picnic table and playing in the backyard of one of their suburban homes. The children are swimming in a blow-up pool. Once a month they meet at a member's home. Today we are in Studio City. The Valley.

The women look too old to be mothers of small children. They are not lesbians. They look like the type of women you'd see at a bowling alley—beefy and plain. Right away, I think: No wonder they're single. They're ugly.

The host of today's gathering stands up to greet me. She says, "You must be Andrea. Welcome to SMC." I stare at her blankly. "Single Mothers by Choice," she says.

"Thanks," I say.

All the women welcome me at once: "Hello, Andrea." "Good to have you, Andrea." "Andrea, nice to meet you." "Andrea, please sit down." This is how I imagine AA meetings.

I sit down at the picnic table. The woman to my left sits with her 4-year-old daughter on her lap. She adopted her at birth, at age 45. She tells me she's thrilled to be a mom. "You have so much to look forward to," she says. "You're gonna relive your childhood. Like in the car, we always sing the Village People." She starts singing "YMCA" while making the letters over her head with her arms. She bats and squints her eyes, creating deep lines that lead to her temples. This woman is so enthusiastic she scares me.

I get up from the table and go over to watch the children. A woman named Peggy stands next to me and points out her daughter. She says, "We do everything together. I take her to restaurants. Last night we saw *Finding Nemo*. It's like I have a partner."

I say nothing. This is my greatest fear—making my child my partner. A kid can't be responsible for meeting the needs of its parent. I need a lover.

I fear mothers make their daughters their best friends and that for single mothers the urge could be even stronger. My mother, although she was married to my father and even with two children, leaned heavily on me, her only daughter. She still does.

Last night, on the phone, she said, "I am so lonesome without you. I connect more with you than with anyone else."

"Oh, Jeez, I hope I have a boy," I said.

With a boy maybe we'll have a little more emotional distance. It will be easier, I imagine, to let him be himself and do his own thing, and not expect him to be my confidant.

I sit down at the picnic table again. A platinum-blond woman with a platinum-blond son tells us about her plans to create a full sibling. She has only two sperm vials of her donor left, and at her age, 42, her doctor recommends not waiting much longer. She's preparing for in vitro fertilization, a process which I learn costs $10,000 and requires harvesting her eggs after a month of injecting hormone shots into her ass. She is excited. She will begin injections next week.

The platinum blonde asks me how I got pregnant. I say, "The Cryobank, sperm donor 3342."

She says, "You really shouldn't tell people your donor number."

"I shouldn't?"

"Well, it might make someone uncomfortable if she used the same donor."

"Right," I say. Now I am dying to know everyone's donor number.

A woman just four weeks pregnant tells the group she's been Internet dating. She's met a few nice men who aren't scared away because she's been trying to get pregnant. I wonder what will happen to her SMC membership if she starts dating someone seriously.

I walk out terrified I'm just like these women. Please, no. They seem so happy.

I call Andrea Stern and tell her I'm desperate. I need to go out with lesbians. I ask her if she wants to go to the LA Gay and Lesbian Film Festival. She says she's going with her girlfriend and will get tickets for the three of us.

## WEEK 18, DAY 4

My sperm bank is part of the Iraqi war effort. The California Cryobank is giving soldiers one year of free sperm banking. This morning, on my way to work, I heard on the radio that the U.S. military uses spent uranium as gunpowder, which is strong enough to fire through tanks. When spent uranium explodes it breaks into millions of microscopic pieces that can get into the body and cause terrible health problems, including infertility.

I called the bank. I said, "I don't appreciate you using my money to condone the war."

The Cryobank spokesperson said, "We're not condoning or condemning the war. And we're not using your money."

"By contributing to the war effort you're supporting the war. And you wouldn't be able to give away free bank space if it weren't for your paying customers."

"We're not supporting the war. The military's irresponsible in not telling these boys that they're in danger of becoming infertile. Some of them are so young. We want to help."

I said, "Sounds more like, 'We see you're going to become infertile in this noble war, but don't worry, you can bank your sperm with us.' Sounds like you're using this atrocity as a marketing campaign."

"I'm sorry. We have a difference of opinion, then."

My dad calls, maybe to try to make peace or maybe to insist I invite Monica to my baby shower. I don't know, because I'm so wound up about the Cryobank I don't give him a chance to say anything. I start right in telling him about the radio piece and my conversation with the Cryobank. He doesn't get it. He says, "Andrea, those soldiers are being screwed by the military."

"I know that."

"Well, don't you believe in charity?

"Don't patronize me," I say. "The government should pay the sperm bank to help these soldiers. I shouldn't be paying."

"The government should do a lot of things it doesn't do."

"Yes. At least we can agree on something," I say, and I feel my shoulders relaxing a little bit. "Dad, I'm sorry about the whole Monica thing."

"It's your decision."

"Yeah, thanks. I've got so much work to do, I gotta go."

I can't concentrate on anything to do with work. Now I'm feeling sorry for the soldiers. They probably joined the military to pay for college or for a better chance in life, which is another problem. The military sucks in people who think they have no other opportunities. Maybe my dad's right: The government's the problem; the soldiers are being screwed. I'm so bitchy I don't know what's what anymore.

My brain is foggy. I swear I used to be sharp. I need to raise $60,000 by the end of the year and right now I'm $50,000 short. I don't know what to do. It takes me two weeks to finish a grant proposal when it used to take two days. I'm washed up.

I tell my board of directors I'm leaving. They are six gay men and two childless straight women. Ravi asks me to wait a month to decide, saying maybe I'm grumpy because the first trimester's the hardest. I tell him I'm in the second trimester.

I have been working without pay for five years, which they know. I tell them my plan to raise enough money by the end of the year to hire and pay a new executive director. I have been raising the money alone since we started—a total of $300,000 so far. I ask the board to step up and raise money.

"It's a long shot, I know, especially because foundation funding is tight this year. But if Bike Out can't exist without me, maybe it shouldn't," I say. The prospect of Bike Out folding breaks my heart, but I know I can't carry the organization anymore.

They see that I'm serious and we make plans to create a job description and post the opening for my replacement.

## Week 19

Kate is seeing someone new. This is the second woman she's dated since we broke up 14 months ago. I wasn't sad about the first girl; I was too depressed to care.

I must be feeling better, because the news of a new girl is sending me into despair. I have woken up the last three mornings at 5:30 A.M., dreaming that the new girl is telling me how much she loves Kate. She says she's going to open up and share all of herself.

This is all I ever wanted with Kate. She was the one I wanted to talk to about everything. Every evening, after a day of working from home alone, I would hear the key in the door and my heart would speed up. I felt like a puppy, wagging my tail. She's home! I wanted to jump on her. I probably did. I couldn't wait to tell her the news of my day and to hear the news from the world.

This morning, I get out of bed at 6 and ride my bike to the beach. It helps to watch the surfers. There are only three of them. They are having trouble catching waves.

I sit on the sand and write Kate a letter, which I have no intention of sending:

Dear Kate,

I feel so close to you, even though we haven't spoken in weeks. I understand you now because I'm depressed too. I understand how hard it was for you to call your grandmother, when she was sick. Right now I don't have the energy to call anybody. I'm sorry I was impatient with you then. I'm sorry I said you were selfish. I know you're not.

I'm thinking so much about you probably because you're dating someone else, and I'm desperately afraid I'll lose you for good. And because so much about being pregnant makes me yearn for a partner to share in this and you are so deep in my heart.

I want for you to feel relaxed and loved by someone. That is what you said you wanted. I'm having the hardest time accepting that it can't be me.

I feel better having written the letter. I understand why we didn't work and what we could do now to be perfect partners. We could set aside Sundays for dates, just the two of us. Each week one of us would plan our day's adventure. We could go on walks together after work, so we'd have a chance to talk and get some exercise and unwind. Then Kate could take a bath while I make dinner or we could go out to dinner, like Kate liked to do. I'd give her plenty of space and time to read. I'd enjoy that time, knowing I'd have her attention later.

Then, that night, a miracle happened. At 11:30 P.M. I heard a knock at my door. There she was, so beautiful and natural-looking in her Levi's and black sweater. I said, "Your eyes are bluer than robin's eggs." This was a line from a Joan Baez song Kate introduced me to—Joan is singing to Bob Dylan.

Kate had been working on my side of town and wanted

to sleep over. I hugged her, and even though I'm not sure I believe in God, I was sure God had sent her, so I said, "Kate, will you marry me?"

Kate was tired. She said, "Andrea, come on. No." Before we got into bed, I handed her my letter, and we slept next to each other like we had done for so many years.

### Week 19, day 3

I call Andrea Stern at 4 p.m. to see what time we're going to the film festival tonight. She says she never got the tickets.

### Week 19, day 4

My therapist is telling me I have a tendency to create a fantasy, then to get disappointed by reality, and then to shut down. She says that even with her I acted as if I had a crush for the first few months. Now she says she can feel my disappointment and distance.

I say, "Well I'm not cured, am I? Yeah, I'm disappointed."

She says I did the same thing in jobs and with Kate, to the point of losing her. This sounds true. I am so sad right now. I feel sick with regret. I fucked up and I'm losing Kate forever.

My therapist asks me what my love fantasy is. I wonder why she asks, since isn't fantasizing my problem? But I indulge her. I say: "My fantasy is about family. I want someone to create a home with. I want a partner to share in decisions. I want someone who believes in me and who I believe in, even when she doesn't. I want us to provide the assist to each other, like in volleyball when one partner bumps the ball in the air so the other can smash it away. I want to feel connected and less lonely. I want her to be beautiful and sexy, smart and funny and artistic. I want her to have big boobs." I can't get Kate out of my fantasy.

## WEEK 19, DAY 5

I go to my 20-week doctor appointment. As soon as I see Dr. Martinez I cry. I cannot believe I'm crying in front of someone I barely know and someone I want to impress. I know crying is a natural and important function, nothing to be embarrassed about. I'm mortified. Dr. Martinez hugs me, and I tell her I'm miserable and lonely and that I don't recognize myself at all. I say I hate all my friends. I want my ex-girlfriend back.

She writes me the prescription for Prozac, even though I said I didn't want it. She tells me she would take it if she was depressed, even if she was pregnant. She says depression during pregnancy is very common and underreported, and that it may get worse after the baby is born. She says, "A fetus is the ultimate parasite."

I love her.

I ask if she has kids, and she says no. I'm so surprised. She says she doesn't think she wants to go through this. This is a bad endorsement for pregnancy.

"I don't blame you," I say.

I go to the pharmacy, get the Prozac, and go home. I'm not going to take it, but I keep it by my bed, just in case.

Stephanie calls me. She says she's hungry and needs to talk. I say I'll do my best.

I make a salad and a big pot of spaghetti with turkey meat sauce, and she comes over. Stephanie is impressed and appreciative. It feels good to do something nice for her. God knows, I owe her. She's listened to me work out my relationship issues with Kate for years.

She tells me about a fight she had with her boyfriend. She is on the verge of tears while she tells me that he is incapable of making plans and taking her out to dinner.

"Maybe he doesn't like to eat out," I say.

"Well, then, he could make dinner for us at home. He could make spaghetti, fuck. But he doesn't."

"Maybe he wants you to initiate plans."

"That's bullshit. I need a man who can be a man."

"What kind of sexist shit is that?" I say. We have had this conversation before. Stephanie is very traditional in the roles she sees for men and women and she knows it pisses me off. But she is not in the mood to fight.

"What kind of husband would he be? What kind of father?" she asks. She puts her face in her hands. "He doesn't take care of me the way I need him to. The way you do."

Several years ago, before Stephanie moved to Los Angeles, when we were both home in Miami visiting our families, we spent the night together. We had already spent the whole day together, but we were still up at 2 in the morning talking and not wanting the night to end. We went to the bathroom together to pee, like two girls always do. I got back into bed first. Stephanie came in and lay down on top of me. We hugged, and I thought she was just being affectionate. But she didn't roll off me. We lingered like that, with her face nuzzled into my neck. I could smell her hair—clean and natural. She lifted her head and I looked into her dark eyes. I was inches away from her full lips.

My body tensed up. I tried not to breathe too loud.

I said, "I could kiss you."

"I'm scared," she said, but she didn't move.

"Are you scared because I'm a woman?"

"Yes, and because you're Andrea."

I lost all inhibition and told her about every time I'd wanted to kiss her: when we went to our high school reunion, when I saw her improv show and she played a lesbian, when she took my picture. I had loved and been attracted to Stephanie for ten years, maybe 15. Did she feel this way about me too? At this moment, I didn't really care. It was enough just telling her my feelings. I felt crazy good—alive and elated.

She touched my face and shoulder and ran her hand up and down my arm. "You're so soft and tiny."

"Straight girls always say that," I said. She laughed.

"What would it mean for us to be together?" she asked.

"We don't have to do anything," I said. But Stephanie didn't move.

I leaned in and kissed her.

The kiss was awful: stiff and awkward. Her lips were hard and dry and she kept her mouth wide open, creating air gaps. I pulled away. Maybe she was just nervous. I tried again, but there was no satisfaction in the smooch. No closure and no wetness.

I could listen to her tell me a blow-by-blow description of sex with her boyfriend, and had heard many in our 25-year friendship, but now, I was the boyfriend. The experience was tender and loving, but it was wrong for both of us.

We finish dinner and Stephanie gets up to clear the table. "And I need a solid, healthy adult relationship before I can have a kid. Otherwise it's out of order. For me," she adds.

I am hurt. I can't help thinking she thinks I'm doing this out of order. She has no idea how her opinions affect me.

## WEEK 19, DAY 6

I am leaving for Miami to visit my family in a few hours. I call Andrea Stern, who I haven't seen in weeks. I leave her a message on her answering machine: "Andrea, I'll be away for ten days. Do you even care? I know I pushed you away for a few months, and I'm sorry if that hurt you, but more recently I've tried to get together with you. I wish you would make more of an effort."

Andrea Stern replies in an e-mail:

>Andrea, you are a different person than the one I got to know pretty well in the last year. What I see in you now is a very worried and negative girl.

>I know so much is hormones, but I'm not sure what I'm supposed to do with that. I think what you have chosen to do is hard. I would be a basket case. I feel for you. I also miss you.

>But I feel so ignored by you. You assume I am not there for you, but are you here for me? You are completely focused on yourself and on what you don't get. I say, GIVE. Give, Andrea, give. Give what you want to get.

>Celebrate me. That's the friendship I want. When I met you, you had a fire. Then you lost interest in me, and it all went away. Where did you go?

>I'm glad you brought this up. I'm here to chat if you'd like.

>Love, Andrea.

I write back:

>That was the cruelest, most ungenerous letter I have ever gotten. Yes, I am negative. Yes, I am not the same person I was a year ago. I am so depressed I don't know what to do to help myself.

>If you don't have the insight to see past this and remember who I really am, then I don't have anything else to say, except, don't tell me to give to get. That's insulting.

>Also, I have assumed you are well. I'm sorry that I haven't asked you sincerely how you are feeling. But right now I don't have the energy to listen to the answer.

>Andrea.

## Week 20

Today my pregnancy hit the halfway mark, and I feel pain in my lower back and belly. It started off sporadic, but now the pain is constant and hard to tolerate. I feel it all night.

I call the advice nurse at Kaiser, and she tells me that because of my fibroid, this is what I have to look forward to for the next four and a half months.

My doctor had warned me about the pain caused by fibroids, but I expected to be spared somehow. I get off the phone and my eyes water. This really hurts, but more, I am remembering Robin.

## Week 20, day 2

My father is marrying someone other than my mother. I'm at the reception with Tony and Lisa, except they're drunker than I've seen them since high school, so I'm experiencing the whole thing alone.

While my dad is making a speech, I look over at my brother for support. He's smiling blankly. He looks retarded.

My dad says some shit about choice. How we have no choice but to love our children and our parents, but that this time he's making a choice. It sounds like this is the first time, like maybe he got my mom pregnant and had no choice but to marry her and that maybe he didn't really love her or his children.

Tony and Lisa are lucky; they have no idea what he's saying.

## Week 20, day 3

For my baby shower, Janet has decorated the house with teddy bears everywhere. The tuna fish salad is shaped like a bear on its platter.

I've invited old friends, my high school boyfriend, friends of my mom I've known since I was a baby, my aunts and uncles, and cousins, and my dad and his wife. Todd comes with his wife, who is also pregnant, two weeks ahead of me. She was pregnant when Todd made that stupid evil eye comment.

Men are invited, because I figure this is already a nontraditional baby. My mom and my dad's wife seem to be getting along. They know each other, but this is the first time they've shared the same name.

I sit down with my grandma, who I haven't seen since my grandpa's funeral. She seems to be doing fine. She doesn't cry. Never has. Not even at the funeral, but I don't think she's hiding anything. She's Russian, peasant stock.

I knew that my great-grandmother grew up in Russia in the early 1900s, during the pogroms, but my grandma never mentioned her mother's suffering until a few years ago, when I sat her down with a tape recorder and asked her to recount what she could remember. She told me that her mother fled Russia alone at 16 to escape the brutalization she witnessed in her community: women raped and villages destroyed. She traveled for several weeks on a ship, steerage class, crowded in with hundreds of other people, many throwing up and some even having babies during the journey. Later, after marriage and three children, she got divorced, which was almost unheard of in her community during that generation. My great-grandmother baked bread in New York City to provide for her family.

My grandma learned from her mother that you have to be strong to survive. Maybe this is what they mean by Russian peasant stock—strength and fortitude and stoicism. It's in our blood, inherited from our ancestors.

I ask her how she's doing without Grandpa.

She says, "When you get older, they say it's easier when you lose your husband." She asks me how I'm feeling.

"Shitty," I say.

"Oh, you're experiencing ups and downs."

"No, just downs." As soon as I say this I feel like a heel. Why can't I be strong? Where's my Russian peasant stock?

All eyes turn to me and my belly, and my mom tells a story about going into labor with my older brother. She says she fought with her mother the entire day. Her mother said, *This child is going to be just like you.* My mom replied, *You're cursing me.*

She turns to me and says, "Yep, your child's going to be just like you."

Todd says, "That would be wonderful—look how great Andrea is."

I think Todd's not so bad.

People are being so good to me. I am overwhelmed with so much love and support. I don't deserve it. I am on the verge of tears the entire time.

After most people leave, I tell my dad my gut hurts. I can't really locate the pain, it's just all over. I am not able to get comfortable on the couch. I put my feet up on him, then take them down. Curl up on my side, then put one leg up over the top cushions. He is not used to seeing me like this. I'm not either. He says, "I thought you weren't as upbeat as usual, today."

"I haven't been upbeat in months," I say.

"You should enjoy the pain, since you've been so healthy your whole life."

Enjoy the pain? It's one thing to accept the pain, but enjoy it? Fuck that.

My dad ignores what he doesn't want to deal with. Right now, he doesn't want to deal with me. I say, "Great idea, except it hurts."

## Week 20, day 5
My nieces and I have a date at the beach. My dad and his

wife meet us. This is the life, except today my stomach hurts so bad I can't stand up straight. I try to swim, which doesn't help.

Later, my dad calls me in a panic: "You have to stay with your mother. You're in way too much pain, and I know you're not a complainer. You have to take care of yourself and this baby. You can get the best medical care here."

I say: "Dad, I am a complainer, and my life is in Los Angeles. Also, I know I have a fibroid, and pain was predicted. This is not an emergency."

By the afternoon, the fibroid is all I can think about. I think it's growing into my spine. I'm beside myself, pacing the house like a zoo animal. I think movement might help. I think I might be going crazy. Maybe I already am crazy. Maybe I have cancer.

It's been almost two years since Robin's funeral. Janet and Stephanie and I walked into the synagogue holding hands. No one said anything; we just reached for each other.

In the lobby, someone had put up a collage of pictures pinned to a bulletin board on an easel. There was a picture of Robin with her brothers at the Parrot Jungle when she was about ten years old. They have parrots on their arms and heads. There was one of Gregory and Robin in their New York City apartment on the day he proposed, and one of Robin and her girls, apple-picking, from just a month or so before she died. She looked beautiful.

In the center was a big black and white of Robin alone, looking straight into the camera. Janet whispered, "That was her business school portrait. Robin hated that picture."

We walked through the people. I saw Robin's college roommate. I've known her for years. Hadn't seen her for years. What do I say? "Nice to see you," I said. It was.

Gregory's dad was on crutches and smiling. I heard him say that his wife kicked him out of bed and broke his foot. I always liked him.

Janet and I had taken turns being strong for the six months before Robin died. Janet would say, "It's your turn to call." I'd always protest because I thought she was much better at knowing what to say. But if Janet said it was my turn, I'd call.

The worst was when Robin's dad answered. How do you ask a father who adores his one little girl how she's doing, when you know she's dying? He always sounded a few beats behind, like we were talking long distance in the old days.

Robin's mom, Barbara, was easier to talk to. She had a grace I had not seen in her before. In high school, I thought of Robin more as the mom. Barbara would play coy when asking Robin to do something, which always sounded like she was asking for Robin's permission. But when Robin was dying and I called, Barbara would tell me the details without bullshit.

Robin never answered the phone.

"We have to," I said, and steered us in the direction of Robin's mom. As we approached, Barbara looked past relatives and friends and right into my eyes. She put her arms around all of us and said, "Robin loved you so much."

We went into the chapel and sat down in the back row. The benches were already filling up. There were so many people there I didn't know. Most were remnants of Robin's adult life: young moms and dads, work friends, New Jersey neighbors.

As a kid, I thought about my funeral. Robin and I even talked about it, not that we wanted to die; we just wondered what our funerals would be like and who would come. I counted 328 people and wished I could tell Robin she got a great turnout.

The synagogue was dark and plain, with wood-paneled walls and gray carpet. The room looked like it stank, but it didn't.

I thought of Robin in the synagogue where we grew up. Bet Breira is open and bright, with high ceilings and lots of windows—clear and stained glass. But not brooding stained glass. Ancient rabbis built synagogues without windows, so the congregants wouldn't be distracted. But our rabbi built Bet Breira with a different philosophy. He wanted the sun or the moon to shine in to give his congregants an awareness of God.

But we were in New Jersey and we were not to be distracted.

We spent the next three hours listening to eulogies for our dead friend.

Her dad said she did everything she did with all of her heart. Robin never once told me she loved spending her days in the geriatrics department of a health insurance company.

Gregory said they moved into their dream house together. Robin told me she didn't like the house at first.

Seven people pronounced Gregory and Robin soul mates.

When her sister-in-law said Robin was practical, I finally recognized the person they were talking about. Her sister-in-law said that whenever she had a problem, Robin would give her better advice than anyone. Yes, this was true. Robin had a way of cutting through the emotion, or ignoring it altogether, and solving problems.

Her dad said she never started a fight. That's right. I lost Robin 15 years ago because she didn't fight. But I'm just as guilty. I didn't fight either.

Her dad suggested that if there were more people like Robin, ours would be a peaceful world. I doubt it. There'd just be a bunch more people, bottled up, getting cancer.

Her best friend said she never complained. Her mom said she never complained. Gregory said she never complained. Why not? Why didn't she throw a fucking fit when ten pounds of cancer was scraped out of her insides? When the chemo stopped working? When the doctors cut out her colon and she had to wear a shit bag?

Why didn't she cry hysterically when she thought she might die? Maybe she did, just not to me. Or maybe she was goddamn Russian about it all.

Oh God, maybe I should try to be more like Robin. She died of cancer without a peep, and I am so histrionic; I could kill myself.

Robin's family was comforted by the belief that she lived true to herself and followed her heart. Seems like they knew a different Robin.

I want to remember Robin's beauty too. She was beautiful and complicated, with good and bad, like everyone else. I loved her and I know her funeral was not the place to list her weaknesses, but I still can't reconcile their story with mine.

Everyone's truth is different. The biography is not about the subject, but more about the biographer.

I call Kaiser, though I know it's impossible to get through to my doctor. A nurse answers the phone but says she's busy eating lunch.

"Can I speak to Dr. Martinez?"

"I'll leave a message for her," she says. "But, she'll be out until Friday."

Today is Wednesday. I can't wait until Friday. I can't imagine spending the next four and a half months like this. I want to ask when it will be safe to take the baby out. Forget natural childbirth. I'm ready for a cesarean section today. "Can I leave her a message on her voice mail?"

"No, I'll leave a message for you." It must be this woman's job to keep patients off my doctor's voice mail.

"But without a personal message, she won't know how

urgent this is." My heart speeds up.

"Ma'am, I'm supposed to be at lunch right now; let me have her call you."

I despise this woman. "Please help me, I'm pregnant and in pain." Then my voice cracks and I say, "I'm really scared."

The nurse asks, "What's the matter?"

I tell her I can't tell if I'm having contractions. Some of the pains are short and intense, and there's also a steady ache in my back and stomach. She asks me about my bowel movements, and I tell her I rarely go anymore, and when I do, it's a strain to get anything out.

She suggests I drink warm prune juice and take Tylenol, and if the pain is really bad go to the emergency room.

What's really bad? I know that in the past I've been able to withstand physical pain. In high school, I ran myself into the ground to win a cross-country race. I woke up in the hospital after suffering heatstroke. But now I don't know anymore. Am I a crybaby, or should I go to the hospital?

I take Tylenol and drink a large glass of warm prune juice. Prune juice is about the worst thing I've ever tasted, but within a half hour it makes me move more bowel than I previously thought possible. I feel 15 years younger. I'm not in pain. I feel like I've been pulled over by a cop for speeding and then let go with just a warning.

I'm in my room, where I grew up. My brass bed is the same, the one my mom bought 33 years ago, for $125, which was a lot of money back then. This was my first big-girl bed, and she's been saving it for me, for my little girl.

I am so sad, desperate, for no reason. The baby shower was beautiful, the prune juice is working, what?

My mom comes in and I don't know what triggers it, but I get choked up. She sits down on the side of my bed and touches my leg.

"Don't cry, baby," she says. "You're going to be fine."

I try not to cry. For a second I think: She's right, there's nothing to be sad about. Then fury bubbles up from my insides. I remember the two of us, both in long, curly pigtails. I was probably 4 years old. My mom was younger than I am now. She took me to Jordan Marsh, the department store where we did all of our clothes shopping. Maybe I needed shoes, I don't remember. But I do remember crying. My mom said, "Don't cry, baby." But, I couldn't stop. Then in a harsh voice she seldom used, she said, "Stop it."

I stopped. I wanted to please her.

I hardly remember crying again, except when I got my SATs back. I also never threw up. I was proud of not crying and not throwing up. I thought it meant I was tough.

"Will you leave me alone?" I say.

"Good night." She kisses me on the head before leaving. I lie in bed for a long time, seething, but I don't cry.

## Week 20, day 7

I feel fat and full all day. After dinner I get up from the table and feel a sock in the gut. Doubled over, I go right for the prune juice. Even though it's gross, I'm so thankful I could sing "Hallelujah." Since a glass isn't exactly a scientific measure, I may have overdosed. I welcome this type of complication.

## Week 21

Everyone thinks I'm having a boy. By everyone I mean the waiter at the diner, my grandmother, and my neighbor across the street. I was getting out of my car today when she yelled, "You're having a boy."

At the same moment, a man riding by on a bicycle, talking on his cell phone, screamed out, "You're having a boy."

## Week 21, day 2

My family is involved in an all-out campaign against the names I'm considering: Sebastian and Raphael. My sister-in-law, Lisa, is the worst. She hates my choices and lets me know. She mocks the mothers at the mall in Miami calling after their sons. "Se-bas-ti-an, Se-bas-ti-an," she says with a bad Cuban accent. I didn't realize Lisa was racist. Makes me like the name even more.

Lisa says the only job for a kid named Raphael is hairdresser. I say, "Good, 'cause I'm hoping for a fag."

My mom says she'll accept any name I choose. She will love the child no matter what. But every time we talk, she has new name ideas.

"I met the most beautiful boy who said himself that his name could be for a boy or a girl. Ready?"

"Go ahead," I say. She knows I don't want to box the child into one strict set of gender ideas. She knows I'm against pink and blue.

"Dylan."

"I like it, but it's trendy," I say. "And I don't really want to name my child after Bob Dylan."

"Or Dylan Thomas, even better," she says.

"I don't know who that is." I say.

"A poet. Hey, I forgot to tell you, Sebastian is the name of the crab in the cartoon *The Little Mermaid*."

"Is the crab bad?"

"No, but it's a crab."

## Week 21, day 3

My gums are swollen; another pregnancy side effect. I go to sleep and wake up feeling like the whole side of my face is wounded. What if my teeth are infected and infecting the baby?

I tell Stephanie I'm afraid to go to the dentist. I'm afraid of being around radiation even though my doctor says it's okay after the first trimester.

She says, "You'll probably be okay, even if you don't go. It's not like all mothers are wearing dentures."

That's a good point.

## Week 21, day 4

There is a nice, new feeling down there, especially when I go to the doctor. I think it's a sign of a sex drive.

I can admit I have a huge crush on Elena—Dr. Elena Martinez, my doctor. I haven't felt anything in months. Nothing. Now there's Elena.

She is so sensitive. I remember the first time she touched my knee and said, "Now I'm going to insert the ultrasound."

I remember the first time Kate touched me. I was scared and open and wanting. She reached down and moaned as if I were touching her.

Elena called me the other day. Well, I had called her three times, and she was just returning my calls to tell me to drink warm prune juice. I was so happy to hear her voice. She said pain from constipation can be severe and may feel a lot like contractions, especially if I've never had contractions.

I asked her if my fibroid might be tricking my body into thinking I'm more pregnant than I am and sending me into early labor.

She said, "You're very inventive. But no." I think she likes me.

She gave me her secretary's direct line and told me I could make appointments and reach her quicker this way. She told me not to tell anyone.

I can't wait to see her again. Just 17 more days.

## Week 21, day 5

I haven't heard from Kate since I gave her my letter and asked her to marry me. I know she needs time away from me, time to get to know her new girlfriend. This makes sense. I can grant her that.

Except, I miss her.

It's 4 A.M., and I've been up for at least an hour. What do I do about circumcision? It's so savage, the snipping of the foreskin. But without the snip, the penis looks like an anteater. And may be harder to keep clean. That's probably not true, and foreskin is its natural state. But circumcision is a covenant with God. But I don't care about covenants with God. So why do it to my poor boy and possibly reduce his pleasure forever? How do we know anyway if his pleasure is reduced? It seems like circumcised men feel plenty of pleasure. Maybe it's a good idea to reduce a man's pleasure. Maybe this was God's way of reducing a man's libido so he can focus on the Torah. But then my child is probably not going to study Torah. But I'm still a Jew, and my child is Jewish, and with so much shit that has befallen our people, I need to stand strong and identify proudly. But then am I irreversibly imposing my will on my child?

I can't make this decision on my own. I can't have a child.

It's 6 A.M. Coffee Bean is scratching at the Cheerios box I use to block the cat door because opossums are coming in every night. This is a new development—the opossums in the house—which started about two weeks ago when my neighbor, Flora Chavez, died. Flora lived three houses down, and according to my other neighbor, Flora was feeding the opossums that lived in her backyard. Without Flora, the opossums have nothing to eat. But my neighbor, who has at least six cats, feels bad for them, as she apparently feels bad for all creatures, so she's been putting out dog food in our shared yard.

Opossums seem to like cat food better than dog food, so they're coming inside to get Bean's.

I asked my neighbor to stop. I said, "You're attracting rodents." But she just gave me a look like how could I be so cruel?

I have to move.

It's 10:15 A.M., and I can't get out of bed. I can't open my eyes. I must be in a new phase of pregnancy, one that requires 11 hours of sleep. Maybe there's a gas leak and I'm slowly dying. I open the window.

## WEEK 21, DAY 7

A friend I know from Lesbian Camping invited me to a movie. She walks in the door wearing a full face of makeup. I say, "You're wearing makeup." Since I know her from camping, the makeup is a shock.

She says, "I can't go on a date without makeup."

This is a date? I stand by the front door with my mouth open. I try to maintain composure. I close my mouth. I close the door and lean on it. I feel sick and sad; so sad. How can I go on a date with someone other than Kate? I say, "Excuse me," and go to the bathroom.

I'm sitting on the toilet with the lid down, fully clothed, staring at the bathtub. Kate loves baths. The first time she took a bath, in the claw-foot tub in the big, old house I rented in Washington, DC, she had just broken up with someone she wasn't that into. She said she needed time to get used to the pace of being alone again. I made her dinner and poured her a bath. I brought her a glass of water. She looked beautiful in the tub, like a cherub with soft red lips and rosy cheeks. I wanted to touch her skin. I handed her the water and left her alone.

But I couldn't stay out of the bathroom. I went in again to bring her a candle, and this time she knew I was flirting. Later, she told me that every time she heard me approaching the door, she squeezed her nipples to make her breasts look sexy and perky. When she told me that, I knew I would love her for a very long time.

I stand up, look at myself in the mirror, and even though I know I'm not ready, I say: "Fuck Kate. You can do this."

I walk out of the bathroom. "Ready," I say, and we're out the door.

Her face smells like mothballs and old ladies. I have to crack my window in the car. During the movie, I'm so distracted by the stench I have trouble watching.

While we're having tea, she says, "I'm going to ask you a few questions and then you ask me some."

I answer her questions and then tell her I'm tired.

When she drops me off, I say I'm not ready to date, first true thing I say all night, and walk inside with lightness in my step.

## Week 22

I wake up so depressed I don't know what to do with myself. I call Kate. I cry hard for two hours and she listens, even though she can't understand me most of the conversation. Kate says gently, "When you say you want to get back together with me, I think you're insane."

"I know we didn't work, but I still think we belong together. I'm so sad. I've never felt this terrible."

By the end, Kate gets impatient. "You don't want me. What you want is the fantasy. I have gotten back together with you so many times, and you're never happy when you have me." Then she tells me, over and over, that we will never be together again. She is sick of thinking about us as a couple. She is happy dating other people. I need to talk to other people about this, if this is how I feel.

I call Stephanie after Kate and I hang up. I'm afraid to call, because I know Stephanie doesn't want to hear it. She cut me off a week after Kate and I broke up the first time. She told me flat out: "I don't want to hear any more about you and Kate. We have to have a relationship separate from yours with Kate." It was the harshest thing she ever did, and we didn't talk for a long time. But ultimately I understood. She had been listening to me air my relationship problems for years. She needed to draw a line.

But now, I need to be understood. I need validation. I feel so alone.

Stephanie knows I'm desperate, and she listens as I rehash the whole conversation. Stephanie says, "What you need is someone to put their arms around you when you feel overwhelmed. What you're doing is so overwhelming."

Stephanie starts to cry. She says, "I wish I could be that person for you. I wish I were a lesbian."

I think I'm going to barf. She has said this before. "Don't say that," I say. "It's too dangerous to think of you that way, Steph. I AM a lesbian."

## Week 22, day 2

I write Kate an e-mail:

> I'm sorry for coming undone like that. I know we aren't supposed to be together, and I will never bring it up again. I just want us to be friends like we were before. I know I will soon be able to hear about you and your girlfriend, and I want to know how you are doing, always. You are more than a friend; you are my family, and I'll always think of you that way.
>
> I hope you can understand that I am more afraid than I have ever been in my life. I'm depressed. But I'm not asking you to take care of me. I only wish that you would check up on me every

once in a while and be tender sometimes, because I really need that. If you ever need me, I would do anything for you. I'm really sorry about last night. I love you.

Love, Andrea.

## WEEK 22, DAY 3

My heart is broken, and my refrigerator's broken. Has been broken for a week. My landlord promised me a new one, which is arriving in three days.

I sit down for dinner at the Sunset Grill, alone. I can't bear another meal alone even while I realize that soon I may never have a meal alone again.

## WEEK 22, DAY 4

My friend who's a massage therapist recommends I see a prenatal massage therapist, who recommends I speak to a doula, her friend Dana Ridge. This is the way it works in Los Angeles: Women who are pregnant or who have ever been pregnant know just what you need. You have to call my herbalist, he specializes in morning sickness. Oh, my acupuncturist cured my constipation. My gynecologist is the best in the world. I know the best prenatal yoga teacher. You should try the *Birthing from Within* labor class. Lamaze is out. Have you thought about hypnobirthing?

All this advice is more than I can handle, but because three different women suggest I call Dana Ridge, I do. I don't know what a doula is. Dana explains that she's the mother's helper during birth. A doula is a cross between a nurse and a midwife.

We speak for an hour on the phone, and she tells me about the Hollywood Birth Center, where midwives assist with birth either at the Center or at your house. They bring you a plastic hot tub and you can have your baby underwater.

I've always imagined giving birth this way, with my arms wrapped around other women's shoulders while I push and scream. This is how elephants give birth, with their elephant friends by their sides.

## WEEK 23

My new friend Phyllis, who's a prenatal yoga teacher and the mother of a 7-month-old, shows me pictures of her labor during the birth of her daughter. Dana Ridge and the Hollywood Birth Center assisted her home birth.

In one picture Phyllis is leaning against her husband in the birthing tub. Phyllis tells me gross things happen in the tub. Poo is scooped out with a goldfish net. But all I can think about is being in the tub with Kate. I want to feel her soft body against my back and her strong arms around me.

I ache for Kate's body. Kate and I were like puppies, always cuddling up together. I dream of making love with her again. I long for the smell of her neck: like freshly baked bread. I yearn for the feel of her softness under me. Her body makes me feel vulnerable and, at the same time, safe in the world.

Two weeks before Robin died, Kate sat down next to me on my couch. She looked so young and pretty, like a college girl. Her hair was damp from a shower and it fell loosely around her face. Kate typically pays $8 for a haircut. She paid more for this one.

I had just got off the phone with Janet, who told me more bad news about Robin's condition. Kate asked me how I was feeling, and I remember saying I didn't really feel anything. I told her how strange it was that I was just going to go on with my day as usual, while my friend was experiencing one of her last. Kate patted her chest, motioning for me to lean against her. She hugged me, and it felt warm.

"I wrote Robin a letter. Do you think I should send it?"

"Of course," Kate said, "but don't expect anything in

return. Robin is busy right now. It's like she's packing for a very long journey. She'll bring her letters and her yearbooks, but she won't have time to look through them."

With her hand petting my hair, she gently coaxed the sadness out of me, and I cried really hard.

I asked Kate to check up on me, and I can't believe she hasn't called. This is why we aren't together, because she can't step out of herself for two seconds to help someone else. Not even me, when I need her so badly. She can't stand being asked for something. And I need to be able to ask for what I need.

I fantasize about punching her somewhere it will really hurt, but not cause permanent damage. Maybe the shoulder. No, the nose.

## WEEK 23, DAY 3

My dad calls to say Happy New Year. Tomorrow is the Jewish New Year. My dad has been calling me more lately. I don't expect much from him, so this feels really nice.

I tell him I'm pissed at all of my friends, which I shouldn't say, because I know he thinks friends are limited and that only family will be there in the end. He thinks I spend too much time and put too much stock in friends. I have argued with him before, saying he just doesn't understand me and my life. I've told him that for gay people, people who create alternative families and who are sometimes estranged from their biological families, friends are family. Today I'm not sure who is my family.

"A few people I thought were really good friends I haven't seen in months," I say.

"People have their own lives," he says.

"I know. It pisses me off."

"Aren't you, as much as anyone else, living your own life?"

"Yeah," I say. "It takes one to know one. I see that."

"Family will always be there for you, friends might not."

"I don't feel like family is there for me either. I sent Tony pictures of me weeks ago, and he hasn't even looked at them." Arguing with my dad that family isn't there for me isn't an argument I want to win.

"Did you ask him to look?"

"Of course. He doesn't even care."

"He cares," my dad says.

"It doesn't seem like it."

I'm remembering every single time Tony was an asshole. Like when Kate and I came to town for Rachel's first birthday party and he asked me not to announce that Kate and I were a couple. I said, "What do you think I'm going to do, clink a glass and say, 'Excuse me, everybody, meet my lesbian lover. By the way, we like pussy'?" Or the time, maybe a year after I came out, when Tony set me up on a blind date with one of his fraternity brothers. I went so I could embarrass him. As soon as I sat down with Adam Schlotznick, I said, "I can't date you. I'm a lesbian. Could you let Tony know?"

Now I'm 3,000 miles away, but I want to share this pregnancy as best I can. I want Tony to see how big my belly is. I hate being in California. I wish I were in Miami, closer to my mom and dad and nieces and brother, even if he sucks. I guess my family's better than some of my friends, especially the ones who have ignored me for six months.

I hate that I don't have the nuclear family my dad is talking about. I want a partner.

My brother calls after I get off the phone with my dad. I wonder if my dad called him, but soon realize he didn't. Tony is coming to LA for a few days to go to a conference. He says, "Will you get me a place to stay in Venice?"

I say, "Stay at the Venice Beach House."

"Oh yeah, what's their number?"

"Am I a fucking travel agent? Get it yourself."

"Jesus, what's wrong?"

"Why haven't you looked at my pictures?"

"I forgot," he says.

"Do you ever think about anyone except yourself?"

"Wow, look who's talking."

"What's that supposed to mean?"

"You act like everyone's life should be on hold because you're pregnant. You are so self-centered right now, I barely recognize you."

"You'd recognize me if you'd look at my pictures."

"I'll look at them tonight."

"Don't bother."

## WEEK 23, DAY 5

I wake up at 7 A.M. feeling like I've been shot in the calf with a gun. I'm having a charley horse. But this is no ordinary charley horse. I sit up too fast, forgetting I'm pregnant. For the rest of the day I have sore a back from the sudden movement. My calf is sore too.

## WEEK 24

My calf is still sore from the charley horse. This is a bad joke, another cruel side effect.

I'm in the doctor's office, waiting for Elena. She comes in smiling. She is dressed up under her lab coat, which she wears open. She looks heavier. Her blouse is low-cut and inviting, and I can see her freckled chest and neck and the start of her breasts under a white bra. Her boobs look big and nice. She looks so pretty I want to tell her. She hugs me. She says I look beautiful. I blush.

I've gained 23 pounds. Twenty-three pounds in 24 weeks.

At least my number of weeks pregnant is more than my weight gain. I don't care anymore. And this is probably a firm indication that I don't have cancer. Robin gained six pounds her entire pregnancy. I don't think I'd be gaining at this clip if I had cancer.

Elena says 23 pounds is perfect. She measures my belly, which comes to 24 of some measurement, I think she calls them *sonometers*. She says 24 sonometers is perfect. We listen to the baby's heartbeat, which is such a thrill. All is perfect, she says.

I only have a few questions, which we cover quickly. I tell her that the prune juice is working and thank her again for calling me. I tell her I sneezed and peed in my pants. She laughs hard.

"That's not funny," I say, smiling. "I'm not talking a little trickle. I was holding grocery bags, sneezed twice, and pee shot out through my underwear and through my pants. I'm not ready to be incontinent."

"If you have a laughing attack, you'll lose it all."

"That's fine," I say, "since I never laugh anymore." This is my attempt at flirtation. Maybe she'll think I'm sexy if I'm dark and brooding. "Do you think it'll help to do Kegels?" She gives me a look that means probably not. "This is horrible," I say.

I feel nervous, suddenly. I need to tell her about the Hollywood Birth Center, but I don't want her to feel like I'm two-timing. I blurt it out. "I'm looking into having my baby at the Hollywood Birth Center. Do you think it's safe?"

She puts her hand on my knee and says, "I think that's a really good idea for you."

She understands me.

"Do you think my fibroid will complicate birth?"

"No, I don't. It hasn't grown, and the baby is pushing it back, out of the way of the vagina. You'll be fine."

She gives me a list of questions to ask them: Do they have the ability to resuscitate the baby? Do they have baby warmers? Do they give blood-clotting medications to the mother in case of hemorrhage? I write these questions down. "I've heard very good things about them," she says. "I'll see you in four weeks."

I wish I had more questions; the visit ends too quickly.

Week 24, day 2

Two weeks, and no word from Kate.

# Third Trimester

## Week 25

Today marks the first day of the third trimester—the final trimester. I'm a senior, coasting until graduation. I've done all my homework—next, the exam. Then, of course, the hard part: life in the real world.

So now what? Last night, another charley horse, in the other leg.

## Week 25, day 3

A woman I have just recently met invites me to her family's Passover Seder. I don't think this is a date, although it's hard to know with lesbians and this woman is very pretty. More likely, she's being charitable, inviting me into her home while I'm thousands of miles from my family and in this condition.

Her sister greets me at the door and says, "You must be Stacy's friend. It's so nice to meet you."

I say, "Well, I just met her last week."

Stacy's sister doesn't know how to respond. "Oh," she says. I wish I hadn't said that. Why couldn't I have just said, Yes, I'm Stacy's friend?

Stacy greets me like we've known each other for years and introduces me to her entire family. I sit down next to a hip-looking, 50-something woman who's in from New York. She asks me about my husband.

"I'm a lesbian," I say.

"Oh, I'm sorry for assuming. Is your partner here?"

"I'm doing this alone."

"Wow," she says. Her eyes widen. "Good for you."

"Why?" I say. "Wouldn't it be better for me if I had a partner?"

She is not the first person to respond in this way. Most people are overly impressed that I'm single. This always makes me want to cry.

## WEEK 25, DAY 4

Stephanie and I are hosting a Seder for the second night of Passover. Todd's in town because his wife's parents live in Los Angeles. We have asked him to lead the service, since he is the most religious.

I downloaded a humanist Haggada—the story of Passover that is read during the meal. The traditional Haggada is sexist and refers to God as our father, king of the universe. Our Haggada refers to God as a heavenly spirit. I think this might rile Todd.

Todd has told me before that the Seder and the Sabbath are times for Jews to be together, exclusively. I invite Ravi, whose parents are Hindu but who grew up in America without religion, plus the guy he's dating. This is their third date and this guy's first Seder. Andrea Stern, who is Jewish, brings her Catholic girlfriend. And Stephanie brings her non-Jewish boyfriend.

It takes all of my energy to not invite Kate. Kate grew up Catholic, but we have shared six Seders together. This was our favorite holiday.

Todd takes his leadership role very seriously. There is no Hebrew in our Haggada, but Todd says the prayers in English and Hebrew. I tell him he could be a rabbi and he is proud.

The Seder is nice for the first hour, but soon everyone is hungry and cranky. I am eating matzo the whole time, but everyone else is waiting for the meal. I say, "Todd, two more minutes and I'm serving the soup." He plows ahead, ignoring me.

Ten minutes later I say the service is over. He smiles and says, "Amen, let's eat." As soon as Todd stops, the room becomes very loud. The conversation is fun before it turns political. I hear Todd's voice over everyone else's. "Intifada! What is that? The question itself reveals your shameful bias."

"I just asked how many Palestinians have been killed," Ravi says.

Todd says, "If you think the so-called intifada is anything but the Palestinian Authority's use of murder as a political tool, you're a racist anti-Semite."

Everyone is suddenly quiet.

"Honey, don't label me," Ravi says.

"There was no occupation when Arafat redeployed bus bombings and murdered Jewish teenagers at discos."

Ravi says, "Okay, but I'm saying Israel should also be held accountable."

"Accountable for what?" Todd says.

"I think the matzo balls are a little soggy," I say. I'm afraid of what Todd will say next.

Steph says, "They're perfect."

"What? The killing of Palestinians by their own people because they build weapon factories in apartment buildings?" Todd is yelling now. "Or what, when the PLO openly chopped off the heads of Arabs who obeyed the terms of

Oslo? See, you can't help it, because you're Indian. Ironic, since you've probably experienced racism yourself. But Indians have always been anti-Semitic. Hitler loved you guys. Even the swastika comes from India."

"The swastika was misappropriated. That's bullshit. You're fuckin' crazy," Ravi says and gets up from the table. I get up too and so does Stephanie, and we follow Ravi into the kitchen.

"I'm sorry," I say.

"Hey, it's not you. That guy's a prick," Ravi says.

"He is," Steph says. Now I believe it.

When Todd tries to resume the service, after the meal, everyone says they have to go. I don't blame them. Todd is the last to leave. He cleans up frantically, like he knows he's done something wrong.

On his way out I say, "That was out of line."

"Your friend's an anti-Semite," he says. "You are pure goodness, Andrea, so if you're friends with him, he must have some redeeming qualities."

"Spare me the bullshit flattery," I say. "I can't be friends with you anymore." I hug his wife and tell her I'm sorry and good luck.

"If that's how you feel, okay. But, if you want to talk, I'd be happy to."

"Good-bye, Todd," I say.

## WEEK 25, DAY 5

Everyone seems to be in awe of a pregnant woman, and I agree they should be.

The woman who works at the coffee shop brings me my bagel instead of having me pick it up at the counter like everybody else. She tells me I look great, and I smile. "Thank you," I say.

I look down and notice my belly button is gone. It has flattened out and now looks like a scar. It is a scar.

## Week 26

I read the paper this morning, mostly to check up on Kate. It's terrible having an ex-girlfriend who writes for the *Los Angeles Times*. I have to see her name in the paper all the time and remember that we're no longer together. That instead I am alone and pregnant and about to have a baby, that there are no cobblestone streets, no Spanish olives, no lazy afternoons in the Plaza Mayor practicing my Spanish.

Then I remind myself that at least she's not a TV reporter. Then I'd have to watch TV news, which is such crap. But I would watch it, just to see her face, which is so pretty, and hear how smart she is, but how she had to dumb her story down for her TV audience. That would be intolerable.

Kate's not in the paper today, nor was she yesterday. She must be in a slump. She doesn't do as well without me. Or maybe she's been taking time off to spend with her new girlfriend.

The paper depresses me, with or without a story by Kate. The lead story reports that the Bush Administration is relaxing the Clean Air Act. The technology is available to clean up the smoke that billows out of power plants, but Bush says the plants don't have to use it. This is criminal. Men should not be allowed to be president. They clearly don't care if their fetuses are being poisoned by toxic air.

I want to hurt that smug-faced president.

I don't understand my violent urges. I think it's true what hippie people say: that love and compassion are the only cure for hate. I can't muster love and compassion for this man.

I have always thought that men and women are essentially different. Women are less violent, because we have a connection to life. We know the wonder of nurturing a life inside us. We are incapable of war, although some of us have been socialized to fight. Most couldn't possibly send their children into battle. We are more evolved. We are better than men.

But I am ready to kill. Maybe when women are pregnant, we are hormonally most like men.

Ravi calls to invite me to a barbecue tomorrow. I tell him I'm looking at apartments. My place is too small. "I thought you were going to stay," he says.

"Maybe," I say. "I can't decide."

"You gotta make decisions and stick with 'em. You gotta be a solid example for the kid."

Oh shit. I can't even decide what to eat for dinner. I get off the phone as fast as I can. I'm going to be a terrible mother.

### Week 26, day 4

Tony's coming to town tonight, and he's decided to stay with me. He says he wants to see what it's like living the way I do. This is a slight, for sure, like I'm some kind of vagabond, but I want the company.

I make up the sofa bed because I know Tony's not the type to do any chores. Also, I want to make him feel welcome.

He shows up late. When he sees me he says: "My sister!" There's a wow behind his voice and he's smiling so big. "Smiley" was one of Tony's fraternity nicknames, the name he told my mom. His other name was "Sock."

"You're huge," he says.

"Thanks, I guess."

"You don't look bad."

"You say the nicest things."

We sit across from each other at my two-seater kitchen table. Tony asks to see my pregnancy pictures and looks through my pregnancy photo album and another album of my life in Los Angeles. He asks questions and seems genuinely interested. It is so easy to hang with him even though we haven't spent time alone together in years.

It gets late, so I give Tony a towel and say good-night. My bed is six feet from the sofa bed and I am watching him through the French doors, which are closed now, dividing my room from the living room.

He's looking at something on the floor. Now he's examining the counter that divides his room from the kitchen. He gets two napkins and with one brushes something from the counter top into the other, then brings his findings to me in bed: "Why are there sesame seeds all over the place?"

"Shit," I say. "I think Bean might have worms."

"Oh my god. Take her to the vet."

"I will. I just noticed those today."

Tony showers in his flip-flops and doesn't take them off until he gets into bed. But first he wraps himself up in a sheet, with just his head showing. Tony's wrapped in a deep-purple sheet under his blanket.

"Good night," I say. He mumbles something I can't understand.

## Week 26, day 5

Tonight Tony takes me out to dinner and to a show. He bought the tickets and even got directions to the theater by himself.

He takes my *Hair* CD from the shelf and plays it in the rental car as we drive, I guess to get us in the mood. We know all the words and sing along.

I eat New York sirloin with peppercorn sauce and Tony has lamb chops somewhere around Hollywood and Vine, and then we walk to the Pantages Theatre. I'm enjoying the royal treatment.

We see *The Producers*, one of Tony's favorite musicals; he has seen it several times. On our way out, a TV crew stops us for our reactions to the show. We love fame, so we comply. A woman announcer introduces the segment, then turns the focus on us. I am stuttering, suddenly. Did I like the production? I can't remember.

I start giggling. Tony tries to stay cool. "It was great. Fantastic," he says. "The performances were great."

She urges him to be more specific, and he says, "The set was great and so was the acting, just great." He says *great* a hundred times. He has no idea what he's talking about. I'm laughing now and can tell Tony's about to burst. It's only local news, KCAL 9, but I can't stop laughing and have stepped away from the camera.

Tony says, "What was I going to talk about? What was your question?"

Now I'm crying and laughing and Tony starts to crack up, like we're making fun of the whole thing, but we're not. It's like we're 10 and 12 again. She thanks us and the crew moves on.

As we walk to our car, I'm still bowed over laughing. Tony's laughing too. He doesn't care that I've ruined his Hollywood TV moment. He's used to seeing me laugh like that.

The next day, I take Coffee Bean to the vet and vacuum the house, but Tony won't put his bare feet down on the floor. He sleeps wrapped in a sheet again.

### WEEK 26, DAY 7

I run into some friends—well, they're not really friends, but women I know from the neighborhood—at the corner liquor store while buying milk.

They are three sexy women I haven't seen in six months, who I generally like, and who tell me I look fabulous and that

I should come over anytime. They've heard from my neighbor that I've been having a hard time. They each hug me, and Pesha says, "I really mean this: You can call me anytime if you need anything."

I say, "Thank you, but I probably won't."

"Well, stop by whenever you want—I mean it," she says.

I have nothing else to do tonight, so I go to Pesha's house. She has recently bought a Venice bungalow with two of her friends, and they've built a deck. I want to see what they've built. I feel off, as usual. From what I remember, I used to be cool and social and fun to be around. Not anymore. But as the night goes on, I accept my awkwardness and this helps me relax.

Maggie asks me what names I'm thinking of. I say naming my kid is too hard, and then all three of them take on the challenge.

"Beckett?" Maggie says. She's scanning her bookcase. "Beckett Askowitz." Pesha writes it down.

I think Beckett Askowitz has a good ring to it, but I haven't read any Beckett. I should at least know what *Waiting for Godot* is about before giving the name to my child. I don't say this, though.

Julie says, "Madagascar." She's reading from an atlas.

"Ibsen?" Maggie says. "How about Cyrano?"

Pesha says, "We should interview you and get a sense of what you like. What's your favorite book?"

"*The Bell Jar.*"

"Sylvia Askowitz," Maggie says.

"Too suicidal," Julie says.

"What do you like to do for fun?" Pesha asks.

"Ride my bike."

"What about Schwinn?" Julie says.

"Yeah, maybe for a cat," Maggie says. I agree.

Julie says, "Oh, oh—Zaire."

"What else do you like?" Pesha asks.

"I like women with big boobs." I say.

"I got it," Julie says. "I got the perfect name—Tits Anne. Tits Anne Askowitz."

## WEEK 27

I call Dave and Cynthia, who I haven't seen in weeks. I called a few weeks ago, and no one called me back. Because Dave is the social director of his family, I leave him a message. I start off strong: "Damn it, Dave, you know I'm having a hard time..." Then I get whiny and pitiful. My voice is shaking. I'm so mad at myself, but I go on. "I feel like you don't give a shit about me. You could at least call me back."

## WEEK 27, DAY 2

I want to be done with my job. It is all I can do to show up at 10 A.M. Then I just want to leave at 11 to go to the pool. Today I force myself to stay. I have a $25,000 grant proposal due in five days, and I'm just getting started. I open up the file for the California Endowment.

I'm a half hour into the proposal when Becca, our program director and the only other full-time employee, yells from the other room, "When are you going to get someone in here to hang the bikes and build the shelves?"

We have been in our new office more than a month and still boxes of office supplies are open and spilling onto the floor. The camping gear is in piles. Water bottles and helmets are rolling around under our feet. I walk out and see Becca lugging an extra computer monitor.

"We have to get rid of those," I say. She looks at me as if to say, *Why don't you get rid of them?* But she knows I shouldn't be lifting computers.

"I'm doing everything around here," Becca says. "But if

you're not going to do your job, I'll do it."

She seems to have forgotten I'm her boss.

"You're right," I say.

## WEEK 27, DAY 3

I am so overwhelmed at work today feels like my first day on the job. Becca is out speaking to a gay/straight alliance in a Valley high school. She leaves a note on my keyboard saying she can't send e-mails. I call our computer man. I check my e-mail, and it seems to be working fine. No one new has RSVP'd to the fund-raiser we're having tomorrow.

Ravi calls. This is his first call of the day. I am sure he'll call me at least six more times. He's a little hyper but a very active board member, and I appreciate him. He says, "No one's coming to our cocktail party."

"Did you call the people you invited?"

"I'm working on getting the food," he says.

"Okay, but don't shrug off your calls. I got four new people yesterday and $1,000. The calls work. Talk to you later."

"Let me tell you who's coming and who said no," he says, and starts to run through the list of 100 people.

"Stop. If you have time for this, you have time to make your phone calls. Talk to you later."

Our computer man walks in five minutes later. He was in the neighborhood when he got my message. I'm thinking: Oh no, not now, I have so much to do. Instead I say, "You're awesome. Thanks for stopping by."

If I've learned anything in this job, it's how to kiss ass. When someone does something nice for our organization, it's my job to smile and say thank-you.

I sit him down at Becca's computer and hope he can work independently. He wants to talk about his girlfriend troubles. Because he will fix our computers for free, I listen.

Ravi calls again. He got the food discounted.

The computer man stays until 4. By this time Becca is back. She sits down in front of my desk and asks me for help deciding whether or not to hire another leader for the expedition scheduled to leave in five days. Right away I say yes. She sits and thinks for 20 minutes. I watch her while she thinks. I am so impatient, but I continue to sit quietly. I am her supervisor. I know she needs my help in this way.

Becca goes to the bathroom and the toilet overflows. Ravi calls again to tell me he is pissed at two friends who aren't coming to the party. I check my e-mail and see that one more person is coming. All of my e-mails are coming in twice. Becca's works fine. I am too tired to call our computer man again.

I get nothing done, but I can't stand to be here another minute.

When I get home, all I can do is rent movies, although usually even a movie is too much to pay attention to. Too often I watch *Sex and the City* reruns. But I am done with *Sex and the City*. I have been completely let down.

For months Samantha, Charlotte, Miranda, and Carrie have kept me company. I consider them friends. But tonight that all changed. Miranda was on a sex binge, and the guy she was sleeping with tried to kiss her after going down on her, and she couldn't handle it.

I could tolerate that type of self-hatred in Charlotte, maybe—at least women out there who are repressed and who believe what they've been taught, that vaginas smell like fish, would have someone to relate to. But all the characters agreed that kissing after oral sex was disgusting. I was waiting for Samantha to say the taste of her pussy was sexy. But even Samantha, the biggest television sexpot of our time, acted like her own body was nasty. Fuck that.

I also rented *My Life Without Me*, and oh my god, I didn't

know what I was getting into. I'd heard it was good. It looked good from the cover.

A 24-year-old women with two young daughters goes to the doctor because she thinks she's pregnant. She finds out she has incurable cancer. She doesn't tell her family she's dying, but she records birthday messages for her daughters to be listened to each year until they're 18. I cry so hard. I can't imagine anything sadder than those little girls growing up without their mommy.

I wish she had recorded more. I would. I would go up to 100. I would say, "Hello, my baby. Today you are a hundred years old. Happy birthday. I hope you are feeling well, little one. I hope you know how much I love you..."

A baby always needs its mother. What if I die on my baby? I don't think I will until I'm old and he's old enough to understand it as the natural order of things, but then Robin didn't think she'd die on her babies.

### WEEK 27, DAY 4

At 9 A.M. I'm lying in bed with Bean, who's sitting on top of me begging for scratches behind the ears. My belly is her lookout perch. Kate calls. Her voice pacifies me and erases all the reasons I'm mad at her. I forget why we can't be together.

Kate says, "I miss you. I miss talking to you."

"Me too." I say.

We have a spirited conversation about what's going to happen to California because of the recall election for governor and how embarrassing it is to live here with this movie-star governor.

"What type of person would vote for Schwarzenegger?" I say. "What's wrong with these people?"

"People are sick of big institutions," Kate says. "Not just government, but the LA *Times* was blasted throughout the campaign."

Kate reported that Schwarzenegger had sexually harassed several women. The next day, Schwarzenegger's spokespeople called the story "elementary journalism." Kate took it hard.

"You exposed him, and they were defensive," I say. "Criticizing the reporter was all they had."

"You have a funny perspective," Kate says. "I guess you're right. But being accused of being a bad reporter really hurts."

"Bust their asses."

"That's not my job." Kate says. "All I can do is report the truth."

I love this conversation; we've had it many times. "There is no truth," I say. "Everything about your background, about every reporter's background, disqualifies you from reporting objectively."

"Yes, to some degree, but reporters aren't part of a larger conspiracy."

"They can't help it. Even the choice of what you write about promotes an agenda."

"Reporters don't sit around and plot ways to bring down the republic, or elevate the republic, for that matter."

"Ah, but that's exactly what you do."

"Good grief."

Kate believes that reporters are the public's watchdog. Without reporters, there would be no democracy. I am proud of Kate for her dedication to journalism. And her commitment to truth inspires me, even if there is no such thing.

Kate explains the car tax issue, the main reason Governor Davis was voted out. It wasn't Davis's fault the tax was so high. The law was written before he came into office.

She tells me why Arianna Huffington kept making the connections between California's energy crisis and Dick Cheney. "Most people were like, Why is Arianna talking about Dick Cheney? But Arianna's right," Kate says. "Cheney and companies like Enron are intimately and corruptly involved in power deregulation."

While she's telling me, I am remembering the night we became lovers. It was February, in Washington, but it wasn't cold. Kate was wearing her denim jacket open. We had seen a play and were walking around Dupont Circle, while Kate explained why social services in DC were shutting down. Congress had appointed an intermediate governing review board that stalled all mayoral and city council decisions. Money was held up for months and city contracts went unpaid.

This is the type of smart that goes straight to my pussy.

I tell Kate I want to talk more, but I have to go meet a volunteer at work.

"It's so much fun to talk to you about politics," Kate says. "You get so into it. My new girl doesn't want to talk to me about stuff like this."

"Get rid of her," I say. And then I tell Kate about the fancy cocktail party we're having for Bike Out tonight.

"Why wasn't I invited?"

"One, you've been avoiding me. And two, we're asking people for a thousand dollars, so I thought I'd spare you."

"I'm special," Kate claims. "Remember in the beginning when I was Bike Out's highest donor? I think I gave a hundred dollars. Can I come and give a hundred dollars?"

"I'd love that."

When I get to work, the volunteer is waiting. Becca is talking her into joining us on our next expedition. My brain is tired, so I decide to join her in walking up and down the streets of Santa Monica putting flyers on cars. On one side, the flyer says, "Got an old bike? Donate it to Bike Out." The other side advertises the grand opening of our Recyclery Bike Shop.

After an hour around the neighborhood, I look for a

place to sit down. The baby in my womb feels like a bowl-ing ball. Pee leaks into my underwear. My feet ache, and I am winded.

My volunteer keeps asking if I want to go back. "No, no," I say. "The exercise is good for me."

After two hours, we have dispersed 700 flyers. I am beat.

Becca thinks I'm crazy and tells me to go home and take a nap. "You need to be perky tonight," she says. Becca might be right. I'm feeling my limitations. I go home to take a shower but don't have time to nap.

At 6:30 P.M. Kate shows up at the cocktail party. I haven't seen her in weeks. She is dressed in black pants and a tight black sweater. I tell her she looks slim and beautiful. I am struck by how pretty she is. She seems comfortable, even though she is one of the first guests to arrive.

We hug, and it feels really good. We talk about my belly bumping into hers. She laughs and rubs it, then bends down and kisses my baby. She says, "You look skinny, except for your huge belly."

About 30 people come to the party; half of them I don't know. They are prospective donors and friends of the host. They are men, mostly. Swanky, rich, gay men in sharp button-down shirts. I am perky, for sure. These are good people, in my book. They care enough about gay and lesbian youth to give money.

I am aware of where Kate is during the entire party, like I have a new crush. I want to talk more with her. I want to be near her, as always. I introduce her several times as my ex-girlfriend. She rolls her eyes. "Why do you have to tell everybody everything? Can't you just say, 'This is Kate'?" I smile.

The woman we have just hired to replace me is here, and

right now I am thrilled to hand over my job. This is her first Bike Out assignment. I drag her beside me, and we introduce ourselves as the incoming and outgoing executive directors. She seems well equipped to schmooze and mentally record all instances that require follow-up. Everyone thinks he or she knows just what we need to do to raise money. What a relief to not have to remember everyone's ideas.

My job is almost over. No more having to be nice to everyone.

A few months ago, I raised $200 in one hour selling $2 raffle tickets at an upscale lesbian bar before the manager kicked me out. I left with wads of cash and several phone numbers. Flirting is part of the job. But that night I wouldn't have remembered a single woman's name or even recognized a face. I felt like a whore. Hooray, no more raffle tickets. No more whoring.

We gather in the living room for a presentation. Ravi talks a little about Bike Out and thanks everyone for coming. He introduces Nalee, one of the first Bike Out participants. She tells the group how hard Bike Out expeditions are. How riding up hills is a metaphor for life. How she learned that if she could bike up a 6,000-foot mountain with 40 pounds of gear on her bike, she could do anything. But this wasn't a lesson she learned right away, she says. She went back to drugs and other things she says she won't mention. But she also kept coming back to Bike Out. Nature gave her something nothing else could. Now she's been sober two years and is a wilderness leader with Bike Out and is in college studying to be a teacher. "Bike Out saved my life," she says. "If it can save mine, it can save a lot of people's."

Then Ravi introduces me, saying not only that I built Bike Out alone, but that in the last year I have profoundly shaped his outlook on life. He says I am a light for him and the youth and that I inspire him by my unyielding pursuit of free stuff for this organization. Everyone laughs.

I am so moved I can't speak. I have done this many times, but now I feel frozen. I say, Thank you, and my voice is weak and stilted. My lip is shaking. I thank the other board members and the youth in the room, and then I say that pregnancy has stolen my brain. People laugh.

I remember my role—to ask for money. I say, "Bike Out's highest donor for our entire first year is here tonight. She gave a hundred dollars." I look over at Kate. She has been so generous. "Tonight we're asking for a thousand."

Kate is one of the last to leave the benefit. I walk her to her car and she asks me to join her for a drink at a lesbian bar. I say I have no interest in being around other women when I'm with her. We hug. I walk away and then go back. I want another hug. Kate rubs my belly, and then while looking past me she lets her hand glide over my breasts. She is coy, pretending not to notice. I giggle and say, "Honey, the belly's down here."

We raised $16,000. This was the easiest fund-raiser we have ever done. I have great hope for Bike Out's future without me.

## WEEK 27, DAY 6

I call Kate to thank her for coming to the cocktail party. It's Sunday morning at 11 and she's just getting up.

"I got your message," she says. I can hear in her voice that she's annoyed.

"Okay, let's talk later," I say. I know that when Kate is snappy it's a good idea to get out of her way.

But she goes on. "You left me the most effusive message last night. How am I supposed to feel when I hear that?"

"Happy, that I still love you after all this time."

"Well, stop acting like you want me back."

"I didn't say I wanted you back. I said it was great to see you and that you're so pretty and that it was sexy the way you rubbed my belly when you were saying good-bye. Kate, you were rubbing my tits. Fuck you—it was sexy."

"It's really hard for me to keep boundaries with you," Kate says. "It would be smart for us to not talk for a while, except you're having a baby."

"You're just as bad as I am."

"I know."

After a long pause, Kate says, "Do you have a plan for when the baby comes? It could be really soon. Who's going to take you to the hospital?"

"Hopefully my mom will be here, and she and Bob will take me."

"What if you have the baby early? You have to be prepared."

"Stephanie will take me."

"Stephanie lives forty-five minutes away."

I start to cry, but fight to suppress it. Kate upsets me so much when she predicts the worst. Kate upsets me more than anybody.

I say, "I hope the baby doesn't come early."

"Well, you better ask some friends around Venice to be on call."

"Like who?" She knows I don't feel close to anyone.

"Ask Andrea Stern."

"If the baby's early, I'll call a fucking cab; if it's really early, I'll call 9-1-1."

"Why are you getting upset?"

"Because I'm scared. What do you think? What am I going to do if the baby's early? Yeah, I need help. I want you, but you're not offering."

"I'm sorry. I don't really know what my role should be. I love you, Andrea. I want to help you."

"This is not the type of help I need."

Then she says she wants to come see me as soon as the baby's born. She wants me to tell her when I go into labor so she can be ready. She'll need to get a friend to come with her for support because it's going to be really hard for her.

"Hard for you? Who's having the fucking baby?"

Kate leaves me a message later that night, saying she's sorry. She just wants me to be ready.

Now I have a clenched jaw, which I haven't felt for months. I brought this on. I'm in a fucking holding pattern with Kate, and it's been going on for almost eight years. I want to end this bullshit, this yearning for the scraps of affection I'm seldom thrown. Why do I accept crumbs?

## WEEK 27, DAY 7

I'm at the bank depositing the checks from the cocktail party. This is always a satisfying moment: putting the money away for safekeeping. I start to feel nauseated. I might throw up in line. The woman next to me has a 10-month-old. She asks when I'm due. I tell her I have at least two and a half more months, and she says she thought I was much closer. She thinks I'm about to have the baby right here and now, like in the bank lobby. Instead, I'm about to lose my breakfast in the bank lobby. I make my deposit and go outside for fresh air. Someone is smoking. How can people smoke in Los Angeles?—the air is hardly breathable as it is. I break out in a cold sweat. I am dizzy and scared.

I go home and get into bed. Work will wait. I call the Birth Center, but the voice mail is full. I know I can call any of the midwives on their cell phones, but I don't think this is an emergency and I'm seeing Elena tomorrow. I open *Your Pregnancy Week by Week* to see what could be wrong with me: preeclampsia, hypertension, cancer...

Janet calls right before I fall asleep. She is fired up. Her oldest daughter is talking in full sentences, and her youngest is smiling. She tells me this with so much fury, and then she says, "It's not fair: Robin doesn't get to see her kids grow up."

"Oh god, that's sad," I say. I had thought the worst part was that Robin's children wouldn't have their mother growing up. But Janet is a mom, and she knows what Robin is missing.

## WEEK 28

It's been four weeks since I've seen Elena. While a nurse is taking my blood pressure, Elena passes me in the hall. She smiles. Oh my god, she looks pregnant. I ask the nurse.

"We can't give out medical information," the nurse says. "You have to ask her."

There is no way. Elena told me just a few months ago she didn't want to go through pregnancy. I can't ask a woman if she's pregnant—what if she's just fat?

I ask another nurse, who also tells me she can't give out medical information.

When Elena sees me, she says right away, "Yes, I'm pregnant."

"But you said, 'The fetus is the ultimate parasite.' "

"That's true," she says. "I didn't want this, but my husband really did. We kept flipping coins, and I kept losing." She smiles just enough for her dimple to show. I used to think her dimple was adorable. Now she looks different.

Dr. Martinez is five months pregnant. She was pregnant for most of my pregnancy, and she never told me. I feel side-swiped, like I've been hit in the head with a soccer ball while sitting in the bleachers eating my ice cream. I feel like I did that day in high school when I found a love letter to my boyfriend. The letter was written by my best friend, and I knew it was over between us—her and me.

I call Janet. What a mistake. Her nipples are bleeding and her breasts are so engorged she says she's bigger than Queen Latifah. One of her nipples is infected and oozing something like pus. She's been pumping with the breast pump on that breast and feeding directly with the other, otherwise she'll get uneven.

"It's a nightmare," she says. "I'm a cow."

"I give you permission to stop breast-feeding," I say.

"Thanks," she says, "but there is so much pressure to do this for at least three months."

"Oh, whatever. We weren't breast-fed." I remind myself of my mom, who loves to tell me how she smoked and drank throughout her pregnancies. I tell this to Janet.

"Listen," Janet says, "compared to having the baby, your life right now is like relaxing in the sun at the beach."

"Oh, shit."

### WEEK 28, DAY 3

I have finally met a woman who admits she hates being pregnant. We're sitting next to each other at a dinner party. She is about as pregnant as I am. She says, without moving her lips, "Don't tell anyone, but I'm miserable."

"Oh, I'm going to tell everyone," I say. "This is my mission."

### WEEK 28, DAY 4

My neighbor, who I usually think is full of shit, came over yesterday to shoot the breeze. Even though I'm opposed to bullshit chit-chat, I had nothing better to do, so we talked. She asked me if I needed anything. I said, "Yeah, my bras are too tight and my underwear's too tight. It's impossible to find giant-sized bikini underwear."

Today my neighbor does the nicest thing anyone's ever done

for me. She comes over with three of the biggest pairs of underwear I've ever seen. The underwear is also stretchy, just what I need to fit over my big, fat ass.

She then pulls out two bras, two sizes bigger than my usual size. "Thirty-eight C, really?" I say.

"You're huge," she says. She's right. They fit. Wearing the bras is like wearing a back brace or some kind of S/M harness.

I feel so depressed when she leaves, but it's not the queen sizes that send me under. I can't help wishing Kate was here getting me fat-girl underwear.

I lie in bed sobbing and thinking how pathetic I am and how I am so sick of myself I could throw up, even though the morning sickness has passed. Here I have the best life in the world. I have everything I've always wanted. I'm pregnant and healthy. I have friends and family who love me. I have money and a room of my own. And all I can do is obsess about the one thing I don't have.

I need to think about people with real problems. I obviously need to get out of my goddamn head and do some volunteer work. Wait, I do do volunteer work. I've been building a charity for five years with no pay. My entire life is volunteer work.

Now I feel righteous. My feelings are valid. Fuck this, I'm allowed to be miserable. It's all relative anyway. I know I'm not working two jobs struggling to keep food on the table for six kids. I know I'm not in prison for life for a crime I didn't commit. I know I'm not dying of cancer. Still, I'm miserable.

I decide to throw myself a pity party. I sit up in bed and jot down ideas. Food: mashed potatoes, macaroni and cheese, ice cream, chocolates—comfort foods. Dress: black clothes only. Music: a violin player.

At some point in the evening I'll tap a spoon against a glass. I'll say: "I have asked you all here tonight to take part in my pity party, because I have felt extremely sorry for myself for the last six months. This is not a cry for help, I don't think. And it isn't an attempt to make fun of myself, because that would be too joyous. There will be absolutely no cheering up at this party. I did not ask you here to cheer me up. Just to bear witness. And in case you have been out of my life for the last six months, as most of you have, which has pissed me off, although I don't blame you, I have compiled a list of the top ten reasons why I pity myself:

10. I'm single.
9. I'm having a baby alone.
8. I hate my friends.
7. I pee in my pants when I sneeze.
6. I have to drink warm prune juice every day.
5. I've gained 28 pounds.
4. I wear hideous, fat-girl underwear.
3. I can smell your deodorant.
2. I'm pregnant, and it won't go away for 12 more weeks.
1. I could go my entire pregnancy, including conception, without having sex.

"Thank you for coming. Do not have fun."

I go to sleep smiling.

## WEEK 28, DAY 6

Today is my last therapy session. Planting seeds was the only good advice I got from my therapist, and now my garden looks like shit. The lavender is slumped over and gray, like an old man. And that is more than I can say about the mint and sage. There are no signs of mint and sage in my garden. Must have died without me looking. The only seed I planted that has come to life is the cat grass, and Coffee Bean has no interest in it. I'm quitting.

I'm sick of going every week and listening to myself spew the same sorry-ass shit about how I fucked up with Kate and what a terrible mom I'm going to be. And talking about Kate just keeps the pain alive. I have to let her go.

"Treat me like a cat," Kate once said. "Let me come to you." Yes, she's a cat, my Kate. She's a lion with a wild blond mane and big teeth. Even the space from her nose to her lip creases deeply, like a cat. Kate lies in the sun. She accepts petting, but only to a point. Too much and she'll split. She is both a fierce lion and a purring kitty.

Is the cat the pursuer or the pursued? Both. The cat is in perfect balance with what she wants and can handle. I respect Kate for that.

But, I'm a cat too. I need to press my head against someone when I want affection. I need to lie back and entice a lover to touch me.

Last week I told my therapist I'm leaving. She suggested I may have commitment issues. "There is no way out of this one," I said, pointing to my belly. I bet she felt sorry after that.

I wanted to leave and never talk to her again, but she insisted on one last closure session, which I know is common therapy practice, but which seems absurd. I almost said: *Listen, if you want to talk about me leaving, you can pay me a hundred and twenty-five dollars.* Instead I just show up because I have not yet learned to fully assert myself. I was working on that in therapy.

She says, "I feel as if you didn't consider me when you said you were leaving." My therapist is of the school that believes that the therapy dynamic inside mirrors the outside. She loves to talk about our relationship.

"Well, I'm not considering you," I say. "This is my therapy." We have talked about how strange and one-sided I think therapy is, because it's a relationship in exchange for money. How sad and lonely and arid, just like Los Angeles, paying for friendship feels. I don't want to get into that again today.

She says, "You aren't the only person in this relationship."

"Well, if you're saying I'm self-centered, how do I get better?"

"You become conscious of it and then work on it and then little by little you learn a different way of being around it. But with the time we have left we can't even scratch the surface."

We have been scratching the surface of this and everything else for two years, which is why I'm sick of therapy.

I think she's bitter I'm leaving. I want to talk to her about her attitude, but this is my therapy dollar. Instead, I sit there for ten minutes. I am watching the clock. She doesn't say anything. She is also from the school that believes that silence in therapy is therapeutic.

I'm getting sleepy. I want to be in bed, but I have 20 minutes left. I say, "Do you mind if I lie down?" She shakes her head, no. At ten till the hour she wakes me. "We have to stop," she says.

## WEEK 29

I feel lighter since dropping therapy, though I've gained 29 pounds.

Stephanie meets me for dinner. I eat a lot.

I mention to Stephanie that I haven't complained about how fat I am in several weeks. She nods. I tell her I have a new perspective, that most women are too thin. I tell Stephanie she's too thin. I'll never wear her size again.

## WEEK 29, DAY 2

I'm going to yoga again. Last Sunday I woke up at 7 A.M. to eat a little bit before the nine o'clock class, when I could easily have slept past 10. If I don't eat, the heartburn is unbearable. I've woken up early for two weeks now. This is dedication.

All the women I talk to in prenatal yoga love being pregnant. But then, they're yoga women. But then, I'm going to yoga, so that makes me a yoga woman. But I'm not like them. I don't wear a yoga outfit.

The class is full. There are 25 pre- and postnatal women at different stages, plus three babies. The moms are an inspiration; they've made it to the other side.

This is one of the hardest classes I've ever taken. We do Downward Dog and Plank and even the Reverse Push-Up, over and over. I laugh every time we go into Warrior One. There is no way I can get my leg up to the front of the mat in one step. My belly is totally in the way. The teacher walks by to adjust me. I say, "Uh, don't you see I'm pregnant?" I'm serious, but she laughs.

Our teacher had two kids, so I guess she knows what she's doing. Now she's tight as a guitar string and probably weighs 100 pounds. She gives me hope for the future. And I feel like I'm in training for something important.

## Week 29, day 3

I go to the Hollywood Birth Center for my first appointment. I meet the midwife who started the Birth Center four years ago and Dana, the doula I spoke to on the phone.

The three of us sit on a bed in one of the birthing rooms like we're old friends. I ask all the questions Dr. Martinez gave me plus some of my own. What happens if the baby's under duress? What if I need an episiotomy? If my vagina tears, do they sew me up? What if I really want an epidural? How often do deliveries end up at the hospital? How long does it take to get to the hospital? Have any babies ever died here? Have any moms ever died?

They answer all my questions. The midwife tells me she

knows of one baby who died during a home birth, but not a birth she assisted. She says, "Sometimes terrible things happen. This baby wasn't able to breathe on its own. But mostly babies know how to be born." She is very pretty, with long blond hair and deep dimples. She's wearing lipstick and I am surprised. These women aren't stereotypical hippie women, like I expected. They are simply nice, competent women who care about women.

About 10 percent of the births they assist end up in the hospital because they are very cautious and don't wait until there's a serious problem. If the heartbeat goes down and it doesn't return to normal right away, they call an ambulance. Neither woman has seen a mother die in 11 years of practice. No babies have died at the Birth Center.

We talk for two hours. They seem genuinely interested in how I feel. They even seem to like me. I fall in love with them.

In the car, right in the middle of my steering wheel, I put a bright orange sticker with the word KEGEL in bold black letters. The Birth Center women believe in Kegels—the tightening and releasing of the vagina—and gave me stickers to put in strategic places to remind me to do them as often as possible. Kegels will reduce the possibility of my bladder falling into my vagina after my baby is born—one of pregnancy's aftereffects. The Kegels should also help reduce the amount of pee leakage I'm currently experiencing.

Meeting the women at the Birth Center reminds me of how I felt 13 years ago when I had a crush on the first woman I ever loved. Life was opening up in a whole new way. I am reminiscent of that young Andrea, open and trusting. I want to give birth that way. I Kegel the entire drive home.

There's a message from Kate on my answering machine. I don't call her back. I make a gigantic stir-fry with broccoli and tofu to feed my baby. And a cake from a mix to feed myself. I reread part of *A Room of One's Own*, which always inspires me, and eat vegetables and cake. For the first time in months I go to sleep feeling like good things are coming up.

## WEEK 29, DAY 4

I might be feeling better, but I'm afraid to say. I don't want to put a hex on it. But I'm starting to look forward to certain things, like birth. Maybe the Hollywood Birth Center will be a way for me to make this pregnancy more the experience I imagined it would be. Maybe birth will be different. Maybe it will even be fun.

I can remember the one good pregnancy side effect: My hair is fuller.

## WEEK 29, DAY 6

My baby wakes me at 7 A.M. playing the drums. He's got good rhythm, a steady beat to the right of my belly button, and an occasional crash on the cymbal. It's weird and wonderful, this steady beat. I can't wait to meet this brilliant musician.

I hear the garbage truck. Sounds like it's parked outside my window. Garbage trucks expel a lot of exhaust. Smells like it's parked outside my window.

Los Angeles is experiencing the worst air in six years. This and the garbage truck outside my window can't be good for my baby. I imagine carbon monoxide and ozone are coming into my bedroom. Smells like burnt tires. I hear a bus go by. Now, that's a breath of fresh air.

This has got to be dangerous, but then Serena and Venus Williams grew up playing tennis here, and they don't seem to exhibit signs of failure to thrive.

I can't remember a day of rain since I got pregnant. We need rain. Maybe I'll name my child Rain.

Stephanie calls while I'm asphyxiating my baby right from my bed. She and I were thinking of moving in together. On Saturday, we looked at a three-bedroom house on a walk street in Venice. There was a garage, which Stephanie could use as a photo studio or darkroom. There was a giant kitchen and a backyard and even a little bathtub for the baby. It was too expensive for me alone, but with Stephanie, we could afford it. I could see us there, Stephanie and me and the baby.

Stephanie considered it for the past few days, and now she tells me no. She's afraid she'll get swallowed up in my world, especially when the baby comes.

## WEEK 29, DAY 7

First thing in the morning, my neighbor is over here saying she wants to help with a baby shower.

"I already had a shower," I say.

"Yeah, but not with your LA friends. We were all talking about it last night: Pesha, Maggie, and I."

"Are they my friends?"

"Yes, they're your friends."

"They're really not," I say. "I've seen them once since I've been pregnant. But at least I don't hate them like I hate my real friends."

"You're a crazy bitch," my neighbor says, but she doesn't say it mean. "Come on. When was the last time you were surrounded by your girlfriends?"

"Can't remember. That's my point."

## WEEK 30

I have an appointment at the Birth Center. For $3,750, the Birth Center is giving me a way to have my baby on my terms. I'm afraid of the pain, of course, but natural birth, with other women there for support, is the way women have been having children since the beginning of time. I want to be a part of that lineage.

Alex is my primary caretaker today. She looks very young and wears two thick blond braids that fall to her hips. She is the only woman at the Birth Center who looks earthy-crunchy. She is relaxed and takes her time answering my questions, which astonishes me. These women are not hurried. They take care of me.

She takes my pulse and blood pressure and tells me what she finds: 110 over 70. Pulse: 76, 16 beats faster than it used to be. The nurses at Kaiser take my vitals and don't tell me what they are. When I ask, they act like they're in pain before telling me.

Alex has me lie down, and we listen to my baby's heart. Sounds like a galloping horse. "Hi there, baby," I say.

I ask her if she's had children. "Not yet," she says. I tell her it's hell, and she looks at me with no expression.

Then I try to be funny. I say, "Do you think epidurals have contributed to overpopulation?"

She says: "Epidurals are used in the global North, where population rates are falling. Overpopulation is afflicting Africa, for example, where they don't have widespread access to epidurals."

Alex is a stick in the mud. She opens my chart and starts to ask questions.

"What vitamins are you taking?"

"The Kaiser prenatals."

"Are they pink?"

"I think so. Does that mean I'm having a girl?"

She says, "They're filled with chemicals and dyes. Your body doesn't respond well to synthetic vitamins."

I say, "I tried natural vitamins, and I didn't poo for a week, and I could barely stand up straight from the pain."

"I can give you constipation remedies."

"I know about raw apple cider vinegar in water, but that's okay. The prune juice is working. Anyway, I'm too overwhelmed to do one more thing."

"Well, natural food vitamins are the only vitamins the body understands," she says. She doesn't seem to understand.

"It says here you're having trouble holding urine."

"Yeah, I pee every time I sneeze. I'm gonna start wearing Depends." Alex doesn't even crack a smile, which makes me think maybe I should wear Depends.

"Are you doing your Kegels?"

"I hate Kegels," I say.

"Well, let me teach you a way to make them fun." I think she's about to make a joke.

"As you squeeze, say, *I love my body*, four counts, hold." She's not joking. "Notice your vaginal area tighten, now tighten your anus and even your abdomen, *I love my body*, squeeze a little harder, as we release, let's say it together, *I love my body*. Good."

"That does make it fun," I say.

"How are you sleeping?"

"Not so well. I wake up in the middle of the night freaking out about circumcision."

"You shouldn't do it," she says. She gets up and pulls several articles out of a filing cabinet. "Read as much as you can about how barbaric it is."

"Do you have any articles about the benefits of circumcision?"

"No, I don't think there are any."

"Well, I'm Jewish. The issue for me is about identity. Similar to being out as a lesbian. And circumcision marks a Jewish boy."

"I understand," she says.

"Are you Jewish?" I know she's not a lesbian.

"No," she says.

"Then you don't understand."

## Week 30, day 2

"I'm finding it difficult to get laid," I say.

Ravi, who has had more sex than anyone I know, says, "Oh, you're back."

I say, "I'm back more than ever."

"Plenty of people would want to have sex with you, especially when you're pregnant."

"Who?"

## Week 30, day 3

My downstairs neighbor at work, who's a professional photographer, asks me to pose for a book he's doing on pregnant women. He shows me his pictures, which are stunning and unique, just bellies mostly.

He and his assistant set up lights in my office. He is confident as he snaps my picture. He tells me how to stand or turn. He talks about how beautiful pregnant women are, how beautiful I am. I take off my clothes.

I have known him for more than a year and always thought he was a friendly guy. He is very good-looking: black with light skin and big dark eyes and long eyelashes. He has a straight nose and full lips, with perfect white teeth. His head is shaved, which makes him look more like a boy than a man. He is only 26.

He chats a little but never stops shooting. I tell him pregnancy is hard. He nods. I start to think he's sexy.

"Who takes care of you?" he says.

"I do."

"Who rubs you down?"

"No one."

He puts his camera down and says, "Don't be shy to call me."

I go home and call Ravi. "I'm going to have sex," I say.

"With who?"

170

"The photographer man at my office."

"Uh, you're a lesbian."

"That doesn't mean I can't have sex with a man. What should I make him for dinner?"

Ravi suggests pasta primavera. "And don't forget to play the CD."

Several months ago, when Ravi was Internet dating, he gave me his secret weapon in case I ever needed to use it. "This CD is too potent to name," he said. "By the fifth song it's guaranteed to get anybody to take his clothes off."

## Week 30, day 4

I call the photographer, and he comes over. He brings oil and lotion, for different parts of the body. He seems to know massage.

We eat dinner. I don't think he likes the primavera. He is quiet. I think maybe he's nervous. I ask him if he has a girl-friend or a boyfriend.

He says he only dates women, but that he's single. "I don't want a girlfriend. I'm focused on work."

"But don't you want love and sex?"

"I have two girls who give me head whenever I want."

"Do you go down on them?"

"No."

"Why not?"

"They just do it for me to keep me out of trouble."

"What kind of trouble?"

"You know."

"No."

After dinner he wants to get right to the massage. "What should I wear?" I say.

He says, "Nothing. I've already seen you naked."

True, but now I'm nervous to be alone with him. I can hear my neighbors talking, so I think if he gets psycho, I'll scream, and they'll come in.

I put the CD on low, put on boxers and a tank top, and lie down on my side on the bed. My belly is too big to lie face down.

He starts with my back, under my shirt. His touch is firm and strong. He uses lavender oil, one scent I love, even while pregnant. I am relaxing. I take off my shirt and he massages my arms, my neck, and my belly really gently. My baby is happy.

He spends a lot of time on my belly, making circles with his warm hands. I watch his hands; they are confident. His fingers are big and lean and pretty. He has very little hair on his latte-colored arms.

His circles get wider and then he runs his hands over my breasts. I am startled. My breath quickens.

I say, "That's nice."

He doesn't say anything but does it again: He circles my belly and then touches my breast slowly and deliberately. One and then the other. I look at his face and find no expression. He is staring at something on the wall. I say, "What are you thinking about?"

"Work," he says.

"You're thinking about work?"

"I have lots to do."

Portishead is playing on the CD. Slow, rhythmic bass. "Is this sexy to you?" I ask.

"Do I want to have sex with you?"

"Well, that's not what I asked, but do you?" I am breathing heavier now. I can't help myself.

"Only if you really want me to."

"No, I don't," I say. I don't want to. This guy's creepy. "But we could do other things."

"Like what?" I look him up and down. His shoulders are broad, like a swimmer's. His muscles show through his tight, white T-shirt. I look to see if he has a bulge in his jeans, but

I can't tell. He is barefoot.

"Well, why don't you take your shirt off?"

"No, this is for you," he says.

He then spends 45 minutes massaging my feet and legs. He takes several minutes with my toes and works his way, very slowly, over my ankles and calves. He rubs my knees and thighs and presses hard against my hip and then my butt. His hands are inside my boxers, making circles on my butt the way he did my belly, and I am breathing heavy. I take off my boxers.

He lowers me onto my back, spreads my legs open, and slowly kneads the insides of my thighs with both hands. He is rubbing and squeezing the soft flesh just below my groin. I arch up to receive him, but he moves his hands down. I raise my hips and he strokes me. I hear myself moan and this embarrasses me.

When he moves away, I arch my back and he returns. I move my hips up and down. I am begging. Finally, he puts his fingers inside me and I move back and forth on his agile fingers. I am getting the most full-body massage I've ever gotten.

I ask again, "Now do you think this is sexy?"

"It's pretty," he says. "Your kitty is pretty."

When the CD ends, he says, "Okay, I gotta go." He leaves quickly.

I lie there awake, alone, thinking about being touched by anyone, even a strange black man who doesn't want me. I take out my Pocket Rocket, which I keep in the drawer of my night table in case of emergencies, and, surrounded by the scent of lavender, make myself come before falling asleep.

WEEK 30, DAY 6

An old friend, Frank, e-mails me to tell me about the lesbian sex scene in *Caligula*. I think he's hitting on me. I know Frank has a free and open philosophy about sex. I am seduced by his philosophy. It doesn't take much to seduce me.

I had heard *Caligula* was disturbing, so I e-mail back, "*Caligula* might be too much for a girl in my condition. Why don't you pick up something else X-rated and come over?"

When he e-mails back he doesn't mention my proposition. I thought I had been seductive and coy.

I e-mail again: "Frank, I'm inviting you over for sex or whatever."

He e-mails: "Oh my god. A sexy, pregnant lesbian. I am one lucky motherfucker. I can't, I can't! I'm trying to be monogamous right now. This is terrible timing. Thank you."

I thought men were easy.


I go to a lesbian singles mixer, thinking I should stick to what I know and like best.

I approach the woman at the welcome table, which is set up in the backyard of someone's house in Culver City. She looks up and says, "This is a lesbian party."

"I know," I say.

"Well, who's the father?"

"Sperm donor 3342," I say.

I'm thinking: This is bad. If the lesbians don't think I'm a lesbian, how will I get any?

I go inside. It looks like the average age is 60. Everyone's wearing the same red blazer. Even the food is crusty: pigs in blankets and baby quiches. I don't mind going home alone.

## WEEK 30, DAY 7

Today I meet a woman at a café feeding her 2-year-old boy. She says, "You're having a boy. I was the exact same shape. Yep, like a basketball."

What shape do girls take? I wonder.

I finally have a conversation with Alex from the Birth Center. I found myself holding a grudge after my last appointment and making mental lists of everything I don't like about the place. I started seeing them as hippie birth Nazis. I've learned something in therapy and see my pattern here. I've already created a rose-colored fantasy vision of the Birth Center and now that fantasy is dissolving like a relationship after the honeymoon period. So before I get disappointed and decide I hate them, I thought I'd address the issue with Alex straight on.

First I thank her for giving me so much time and attention, because I think I should start with something positive. Then I say I left the appointment feeling disregarded. That I've come to the Birth Center to make the birth process mine instead of going to a hospital where I would be strapped down to a bed on my back and everything would be imposed on me. I say that I had an expectation that she would take care of me, because this is the Birth Center, after all. Because I am trying to take responsibility for my part in feeling disappointed, I say that maybe this is an unfair expectation. I continue to say that there were a few things that happened during our visit that left me feeling not taken care of at all.

"Like what?" she says.

"Like the vitamin conversation."

"Well, I'm a nutrition expert. I've been studying this for six years. I'm just telling you that food-based vitamins are the only ones the body can process."

"You know, Alex, in this case, I think you could shut up about being the expert and show some sensitivity to the pregnant woman. I think that's more important than the vitamins."

"Don't you want to know the truth?"

"No, I really don't care about your truth."

## Week 31, day 4

Janet calls me at work. She says, "Did you get a crib?"

"Not yet."

"Get on it. You need to just go to Babies "R" Us and get a crib, a stroller, at least ten onesies, five gowns, newborn diapers, and wipes. Do you still have the list I sent you?"

Janet had sent me a two-page, single-spaced, two-column list of things I will absolutely need once the baby is born. The list includes: hospital-sized menstrual pads for the six weeks of heavy bleeding to be expected after birth, ice packs for my vaginal wound, as Janet put it, and Lanolin cream, for nipple cracking. It's detailed down to the brand names.

"Jan, what the hell was the shower for?"

"You have to do an inventory."

"I can't talk right now."

"Call me soon."

"Bye."

## Week 32, day 2

I wake up and Bean, my cat, is nowhere. Usually she's asleep on the bed or batting me in the face for food if it's past 6 A.M., but not this morning. When I pour food into her bowl and she doesn't come, I worry. My cat likes her breakfast. I shake the food bag outside, which usually brings her running, but this morning, nothing.

Then I hear a sort of coyote howl and realize Bean is in trouble. I call her name and, like a dog, Bean responds. She is so smart. I call and listen and call and listen, following her voice. I step up onto an old milk crate to look over the back fence, and there she is, my gifted kitty-cat, stuck behind a tall fence in the neighbor's yard.

Any other cat would have been able to climb the fence, which is more like a lattice, but Bean is not very athletic. I go through the neighbor's yard and behind the house and open the gate that's trapping my kitty. I hold her tight, although she squirms to get loose, until we're back inside, and even though cats really aren't supposed to have it, I pour her a bowl of milk. I think I might be a good mom.

## WEEK 32, DAY 3

My back hurts this morning. This is a new side effect. I understand it, since my baby already weighs six pounds. At the Birth Center yesterday, Dana pressed and prodded on my belly and then said, "Six pounds."

She said typically the baby gains half a pound a week in the last few months. I got hot in the cheeks. At this rate, my baby could reach ten pounds by the due date.

How am I going to get it out? I hope I have a super-wide vagina. I certainly will after the birth. I know this isn't sexually ideal for most women, but I think lesbians like a wide, stretched-out vagina on their partner. The more she can shove in there, the more sexual prowess she thinks she has. Maybe someday this will be one of my selling points.

I'm really scared. I can't stand the idea of foreign objects passing in or out of my orifices, like pills down my throat or enemas up my butt or babies through my vagina.

I couldn't get a tampon in for a few years until the day in tenth grade when my period leaked around my pad and all over my yellow pants. I was sitting at my desk during Humanities class when I looked down and noticed blood between my legs. Robin was sitting behind me, and thank God. She let me wrap her Mickey Mouse sweatshirt around my waist to hide the blood.

After class, Robin and I ran for the parking lot and left school. This was an emergency. We went to my house and Robin coached me from outside the bathroom door. "Relax," she said. "The instructions say to relax."

"Great idea."

"Okay, either sit on the toilet and lean forward or crouch down."

"What?"

"Or put one foot on the toilet. Hold the middle of the tampon where the smaller tube fits into the larger tube, and make sure the string is away from your body."

"Duh, I got that."

"Okay, okay. Use your other hand to open your labia." As soon as she said labia, we died laughing.

"Help. I don't have a hole."

"You have to, it's in your labia." We laughed again.

"Stop saying that, I have to concentrate," I said, but I was laughing too hard to get it in.

I'd been in the bathroom a half hour and had gone through half a box of tampons, trying to shove them in, but they wouldn't go. A jar of Vaseline had finger-sized indentations in it where I had dipped each tampon for lube.

Robin came in. She pulled down her shorts and underwear, put one foot up on the toilet, and without using Vaseline, she said, "Like this."

Today I am so tired all I can think about is my bed. I've solved the opossum problem by emptying the cat bowl before I go to sleep, but now Bean is waking me up every morning at 6 A.M. to eat. This is what I have to look forward to, I know. I should stop complaining. With Bean all I have to do is pour food into a bowl and go back to sleep.

Just eight weeks until the baby comes. Unless the baby comes early, which now I fear, because he seems as big as a full-grown man. I need to clean out my closet to make room for baby clothes and empty my desk and get it out of my bedroom, because that's where the crib will go.

I need a crib. Or maybe he'll sleep in the bed with me.

That'll save room. But then there are dependency issues. And I don't mean the baby. How will I ever get him to leave? A 6-year-old sleeping in Mommy's bed just isn't cool.

I need a crib. I need a stroller.

## WEEK 32, DAY 5

My mom calls to tell me I need a baby nurse for a week or two.

"But why, if you'll be here?" I ask.

"Because I get tired," she says. "You should look into it."

"Yes, got it, I'll look into it. Do you think I'll need a crib?"

"Of course. Where will the baby sleep?"

"A lot of babies sleep in bed with their moms," I say. "This is sort of the trend lately."

"You're getting too radical. Get a crib."

## WEEK 32, DAY 6

I'm in my first birthing class at the Hollywood Birth Center. There are seven couples sitting on pillows in a circle. Stephanie is here as my partner and my heart feels so big for her.

As a warm-up exercise, our teacher has us face our partners. With Stephanie's hands on my baby, I am instructed to breathe into her hands. I am hot suddenly. My lip is quivering, and I think Stephanie can tell. I can hardly look at her.

When we introduce ourselves, Stephanie says she has known me for 25 years. I say, "She still likes me," like it's a miracle, and my voice cracks. I'm kidding, but part of me does wonder.

Jen, our teacher, tells the class how wonderful it is that Stephanie is here. "There is so much love in this room tonight," she says. "Thank you all for coming, but especially

Stephanie for being a part of this magical transition for your friend. You probably know her better than most of these husbands know their wives."

All this special attention reminds me how lonely I am.

We partner up with someone we don't know and ask them, "What kind of parent are you?" Brian says he hopes to be like his parents. This answer feels rare and wonderful. It makes me like him. I say I'd like to be like my mom: attentive and supportive and so loving. I tell him how, during high school, she would wake up with me every morning while it was still dark and ride a bike while I jogged to get in shape for whatever sport was in season. I'd get to talk for miles.

When we go around the room, April, who spent six years as a nanny, says something about her child's journey and her eagerness to learn along with her. I decide I don't like her. Nina, who teaches music therapy to mommies with newborns, says she can't wait to support her kid and discover his talents.

I write Steph a note: *Everyone seems so excited to learn from their children, why am I suddenly not able to breathe?* She pats my leg.

Jen says, "You all have answered what kind of parent you will be. But the question was, What kind of parent are you now? You are all parents already, including you, Stephanie."

I'm thinking about how I haven't been playing music to my belly. I know I'm supposed to, in order to make the kid better at math. Or at least to help make math class easier. Or at least to get the kid familiar with music so I have something to soothe him with when he's cranky.

But I'm not like most people. I don't listen to music. I like music, and I love to dance, but I don't automatically turn on the stereo when I come home. I don't even have a stereo, just a boom box and only about 20 CDs.

I did try to play Bach to my baby once. The rhythm is said to mirror the beat of the heart. The music was so irritating

I couldn't listen. I hope my baby was listening. Oh, no. I'm already a strange parent.

Jen asks us to call out concerns we have that we'd like her to cover over the eight-week course.

I ask, "What stuff do we need once the baby's born?"

"All you really *need* are diapers, a blankie, and breasts."

I feel better.

## Week 33

I am up at dawn for the third night in a row after dreaming about Robin. She is well at first, and I see her so clearly: her ears poke through her thin hair, even though she has a perm, like she did in the late '80s. Her face is clear and present, and she is looking at me lovingly.

Later in the dream she is sick, but she looks the same. We both know she's dying, but we don't talk about it. We have the same strong connection we had earlier in the dream—the connection we had in high school.

This morning I feel Kate in my heart, like she is with me. I see Robin in my mind, but I feel Kate. I have felt Kate many times after dreaming about Robin.

My back is aching; I can't get comfortable. I think I'm having Braxton Hicks contractions. These are early false-labor contractions, named after some guys named Braxton and Hicks. I'm not afraid I'm in labor. If I am, if the baby is going to make its way out right here in the bed, praise Allah! I want my body back.

I pull out *Your Pregnancy Week by Week*. I'm obviously having a memory problem, because I don't remember how alarmist this book is. I read about placental abruption: when the placenta separates from the uterus too soon and starves the baby. The book spends four full pages on it, so it must be common, but I've never heard of it. I'm probably having a placental abruption right now, but it doesn't say anything about back pain.

This book sucks. Reading is not helping. The only thing that really helps is my Pocket Rocket. It's the only thing that relaxes me and helps me sleep.

At 10:30 A.M., I am so tired. I don't want to get up, but it hurts to stay in bed. I call Dana at the Birth Center, and she tells me I'm probably having muscle spasms. I ask if she thinks I've been in labor since the pain started days ago, and she says probably not. She advises me to get a massage and to take Tylenol.

## Week 33, day 2

Ravi comes to my rescue today. He helps me transport bicycles. Actually I just stand there while Ravi loads up a pickup truck with dirty old bikes we've been storing for months in a church parking lot. He didn't realize what he was getting into; he doesn't like getting his hands dirty. After two loads, he says, "You're taking me to lunch."

After lunch, he says, "I'm taking you shopping."

I say, "I'm on a shopping strike right now. See, my body's sort of out of shape."

"You're pregnant and beautiful; you need to get out of those rags."

It is true that every day I wear the same beat-up lowrider jeans, size 12, three sizes larger than normal, that I ordered out of a J. Crew catalog. Now I wear them with the button open, so I agree to shop.

The clerk at Mom's the Word on Montana in Santa Monica seems nice enough, although she doesn't have a very good instinct for my style. She brings me tops with built-in boobs, like I hate, but she has a big bowl of candy on the counter. Ravi and I help ourselves. I eat at least five Tootsie Rolls, and

I see Ravi eat a box of Dots and maybe a Tootsie Roll or two. When I go to pay for a pair of black cargo pants and a black long-sleeved shirt that covers my huge bump, I'm thinking I need one more Tootsie Roll. But the bowl is gone. I feel shaky suddenly. "Where's the candy bowl?"

The woman says, "It's bad for your baby to eat too much sugar."

I look at her like a snake about to strike. I say, "It's bad to tell a pregnant woman what's bad for her baby."

## WEEK 33, DAY 3

I have a date tonight. I can't believe it, but this woman who's pretty cute came to the Bike Out cocktail party and thought I was cute, even with this giant belly.

I know I don't have a crush on her, because right away I can tell her deodorant's Tom's of Maine.

We walk from my house to Lilly's on Abbott Kinney, and the whole time I am in a rage against my neighbor who had a yard sale this morning and who said she would sell my desk.

I tell my date how I spent three hours last night cleaning out pens and old letters and how before going to bed my neighbor said she and her husband would come over really early to take my desk. And how I said that would be great, because it's way too heavy for me to lift.

Then how I woke up at 10 A.M. to see my desk, shiny clean, still in my bedroom.

We get seated in the patio next to a fountain. The water trickles and gurgles while I tell my date how I went outside in my pajamas, because I know a yard sale starts early, and said, "Are you guys going to put my desk out here?"

And how my neighbor said, "Sure, we'd love to sell your desk," like it was the first she'd thought of it and like she was about to do me a huge favor. And how all day I've been pissed at everyone in the world for being so self-centered and full of shit.

Now, I know this isn't enjoyable date conversation and I am not putting forth my most charming self, but I continue to tell this story. I'm not even done when the food comes, but she interrupts me to tell me about her crazy neighbor. I have whipped myself into such a frenzy I don't want to talk about any crazy neighbors except mine.

This is when I realize I am just as self-centered as anyone else. More so, probably, that's why I'm such an expert in recognizing self-centeredness in others. But I am not in the mood for self-improvement. I am pregnant. I deserve compensation.

I say, "I hate my neighbors. I'm ready to cut them out forever."

She says, "Yeah, you can't be friends with everyone."

She's way too understanding. I'm not into her.

## WEEK 33, DAY 5

I see Dr. Martinez today. She's still pretty, but it's not the same.

I've gained 35 pounds. Now I know I'm fat.

## WEEK 33, DAY 6

My belly weighs so much it's causing my bed to sag. It's like I'm sleeping in a hammock, except I'm not sleeping at 5 A.M., and I'm not sipping a piña colada either. I'm developing sway-back. Dr. Martinez said the middle of my back hurts because I'm pregnant. I suppose I can trust her diagnosis.

I'm worrying about work. I'm worrying that soon I won't have work. In the meantime, it's impossible to focus.

A volunteer comes in to help fix bikes. We have 47 used bikes making our office look like a junk pile. Our volunteer fixes two in five hours. When he leaves, I look over at Becca, who keeps telling me to take the day off. She is noticing how difficult it is for me to keep my head up off my desk. She says, "I know another mechanic. I'll give you his number."

"No, you," I say.

"Okay, I'll call all the mechanics we know and get them here this weekend."

Thank God for Becca.

## WEEK 33, DAY 7

Tonight's my second pregnancy class at the Hollywood Birth Center. Stephanie can't come.

We watch a movie of a woman giving birth. She is screaming and leaning into her partner, who I assume is her husband. She appears desperate and completely vulnerable, and this man holds her and strokes her head and tells her she's doing a great job. When the baby comes out, I look around and everyone has tears in their eyes.

During the break, April asks me how I'm doing, and I tell her okay but sad. "I'm afraid of labor," I say. "I'm not going to have support like the woman in the movie."

April says, "I don't have that either. I have a partner, but I don't have what it looks like she has."

## WEEK 34

I don't have the superwide vagina I was hoping for. With just six weeks to go, the Birthing Center strongly advises beginning perineal massage to avert ripping the vagina or the need for an episiotomy (cutting the perineum) during childbirth. The area between the vagina and the anus is called the perineum. This is the least pliable tissue within the vaginal region.

Instructions for perineal massage: Wash hands. Apply lubricant. Recommended lubricants include vitamin E, cocoa butter, and extra-virgin olive oil. Place the thumb into the vagina and press back toward the anus until a stinging sensation is felt. Hold the thumb in place for two minutes or until the area becomes numb. For three to four minutes, slowly massage back and forth over the lower half of the vagina, working the lubricant into the tissue.

Perineal massage is best done with a partner. I find it very difficult to lean over my belly and insert the thumb at the proper angle. Instead, I take a backdoor approach and use my middle finger. I press gently toward my anus, and ow. I have a lot of stretching to do.

### WEEK 34, DAY 3

I bump into a guy I know at the grocery store. He says, "Wow, does it feel like you've got a watermelon under your shirt?"

I say, "Yeah, especially at night, trying to sleep."

We do our shopping, and then he's in front of me at the checkout line. He says, "Does it feel like you have a watermelon under your shirt?" I think he doesn't know what else to say.

I say, "You can say that again!"

I buy a watermelon. Some women can't eat one piece of chocolate or they'll eat the whole box. I have this problem with watermelon. I go home and eat the whole thing. I know watermelons come in different sizes, but no watermelon is a single serving. Right now, I feel like I have a watermelon under my shirt.

### WEEK 35, DAY 2

I have only five weeks to go. Only five, maybe three, maybe less.

I'm going to circumcise. I have never known for sure whether I believe in God, but I feel now that I need to have faith. Judaism is my culture, but it's also my faith if I let it be. I trust that having a baby is the right thing, and that we will be okay together. I think I need to trust in something that's in me, but also in something that's larger.

And I'm a wanderer. I'm a single lesbian thousands of miles from home. I want my child to belong to a tribe if he wants to.

I take Kate to Chaya Venice for her birthday. I have one of the best times with her I've ever had.

I tell her I think she needs help; that every other time I've seen her in the last few months she's been nasty. "You don't have to be an alcoholic to act like one," I say. Her mom is a recovering alcoholic. "Maybe an adult children of alcoholics meeting would help you."

She doesn't get defensive. Instead, she listens and wonders with me if a meeting might help her.

Then she tells me about her visit with her mom, who has just been diagnosed with the beginning stages of Alzheimer's. In the last three months, she's lost 20 pounds. Kate thinks she's not remembering to eat.

They were making a puzzle of a tiger, and Kate's mom said, "Tiger, tiger, burning bright." Kate thought she was babbling nonsense, and then her mom said it was a poem. They looked through her mom's poetry books and found the poem, by William Blake.

Kate stops in the middle of telling me this. Her bottom lip curls down. She is trying not to cry, which is not like her. I reach across the table and touch her lip. She cries. She says, "Why am I so messed up?"

I say, "It's okay to be messed up." She laughs a little.

"I don't want to be inconsistent and nasty. If you think that about me, you must know. You know me better than anyone."

"I think you need help," I say. "I know you're not a bad person. You're just hurting."

We talk more about her mom. Kate is angry and guilty and sad. "My mom is leaving me," she says.

WEEK 35, DAY 3

My mom calls as soon as I get to work and says, "The word is, I'm enabling you to live far from home by coming out there for so long."

"Whose word?"

"Well, mine," she says, and we laugh. I am so lucky to have my mom.

"I have to go. I've got work to do."

"I'm sucking hind tit with you," she says.

"What does that mean?"

"I'm saying I'm the runt of the litter. I can't get your attention."

"In less than a month you'll have my attention." I hang up and think that maybe I should have said: *Get used to it, since soon there will be a baby to attend to.*

WEEK 35, DAY 6

At the last minute, Kate invites me to her birthday dinner, so I go.

I just want things to be normal. What a delusion. Lesbians are so fucked up, and I'm their poster girl. If Kate were a man, I would never, ever go to his birthday party after being married to him for six years, and pregnant, and to top it off, see him with his new girlfriend. But because we're girls, we think we can be friends.

Dave picks me up, and we drive to a very hip Mexican restaurant in Silver Lake. He says he's excited to see me. His breath is so foul, like he hasn't eaten for days. He looks pasty and skinny. I open the window, even though it's loud and cold on the freeway. I decide I'm not going to say anything about how disappointed I am about our friendship. I can only fight so much, and then it is what it is.

Dave and I are late. When we walk into the restaurant, Kate's friends stand up one by one to hug me and pat my belly.

They tell me I look beautiful. They say it's great to see me.

Kate and her girlfriend talk a lot, just to each other. Kate seems so interested in her. More interested than she ever seemed in me. I feel sick but tell myself it's good for me to see reality.

I watch and wonder why Kate doesn't love me. I wonder if she ever did. Maybe at the beginning, but she never trusted me. How could she? I was so indecisive. I fucked it up.

Dave says he is sorry we haven't spent more time together. He's been busy with a big job composing a score for a reality television show. "It's tough for me, man, I have to fight for my work," he says. "One day you're in and the next you're not."

"Everyone works too hard," I say.

"Yeah, that's life in America."

"I don't want to live that way."

"Well, I have to. I have to fight to get paid."

"I think you're obsessed with work," I say.

"Well, maybe a little, but I don't want to turn forty and have nothing."

"You have everything already."

The food comes, and he and Cynthia share a burrito, but he is so hungry he eats off my plate and mooches the appetizers in the middle of the table that he didn't order.

I say, "Who gives a shit about someone's work, really? If you don't prioritize people, you'll end up lonely."

"That's not fair. I know you're pissed that I haven't been a better friend, but you know you can call us any time, and we'd love to hang out."

"I called, Dave. I asked you to call me too sometime."

"Andrea, we're just not like that. Who makes plans and drives a half hour?"

"Obviously, not you."

"When you're married, it's different. I put a lot of time into Cyn and my family."

Maybe my dad is right; maybe family really is all you have in the end.

## Week 36

Birth class is hard tonight. We learn that at 36 weeks the baby is ready for a healthy birth. I'm not ready. I'm too tired.

Jen asks each of us to make a list of what comes to mind when we think of labor. I write *baby, relief, pain, ring of fire, charley horse, heartbreak.*

We go around and read out our lists. Liz, who seems cool, like someone I'd be friends with, says, "Orgasm." This is the first I'd heard of the possibility of having an orgasm during labor.

Jen explains that while giving birth we'll be wide open. That we will feel intense emotion and sensation when the baby passes through our sex. She calls the vagina "our sex."

April says, "That's going to happen to me." I roll my eyes.

We do an exercise to help us learn how our bodies and minds react to sensation. Sensation, rather than pain, is the way Jen wants us to think of the feelings we'll have during labor. This sounds like a good idea.

Stephanie's my partner and, like each pair, we get a big bowl of ice. Jen asks the pregnant women to hold the ice in our hands for one minute. My hands start to hurt so badly it's hard to hold on. The pain, like burning, travels up my arms and into my elbows and between my shoulder blades and gets worse and worse before Jen calls stop. She gives us a minute to rest.

We hold the ice ten times, a minute each time, to represent contractions, and each time the sensations get more and more unbearable. Jen has us practice coping skills like visualizing a safe place, moving around, focusing on breathing, or making sounds. Nothing helps.

Partners hold the ice for a few rounds too.

For the finale, we fully submerge both hands in the ice and water for two full minutes. I am on my knees, rocking back and forth. My hands are in ice water in a metal bowl. Liz screams out, "You gotta be crazy." I hear other women moan. I want to take my hands out. I feel like throwing up.

Steph gets on her hands and knees in front of me. I press my face into her shoulder; her face is pressed into my shoulder, like cats. When I try to pull my hands out, she covers them with one of hers. Stephanie is in the ice too. Her other hand is holding my back strong. She can tell I need to be held. She says, "You can do this."

When it's over, I hug Stephanie tight for a long time. I feel more love for her than I've ever felt for anyone.

## WEEK 36, DAY 3

I make the mistake of telling my mom I'm struggling with circumcision.

"What's the struggle?" she says.

"Well, I think it's not necessary."

"Andrea, yucky stuff gets caught in there and it gets stinky."

"How do you know that?"

"My hairdresser told me."

"I don't think so, and think of all the stuff that can get caught in a vagina."

"That's not nice. Andrea, if this child is going to be Jewish, he needs to be circumcised."

"Why? It's not like we keep kosher or practice any of the other Jewish laws."

"Abraham was asked by God to sacrifice his son."

"Mom, this isn't your best argument."

She agrees and then says, "Okay, but boys look at each other when they pee or change clothes, and you don't want your boy to feel strange."

"That's true."

WEEK 36, DAY 4

Thirty-four people are in my tiny living room giving me gifts for my baby, even though I insisted I didn't want another shower. Stephanie planned the whole thing, as if she hasn't done enough, and my neighbor made the food from scratch. She brought over a delicate tea set and dressed the table in a lacy cloth. It is all so lovely.

We are eating quiches and scones, and I am opening presents. I feel lucky. My baby got adorable outfits, including a black onesie that says "Hand over the tit and no one gets hurt." He got booties and books, and Kate got him a stuffed doll that's really for me, because it's wearing a grass skirt and a coconut bra.

Eight years ago, before Kate and I became lovers, I was hanging out with a bunch of friends in a bar. Kate had just returned from a trip to Hawaii and came into the bar holding a coconut bra and a grass skirt. She handed them to me and said, "You're the only person I can think of who would wear these." She liked me.

When everyone leaves, I cuddle up with Coffee Bean to take a nap. I feel full and content. Before I fall asleep, the woman I had a date with, the nice woman who listened to me complain for two hours, calls to make another dinner plan. I say, "I don't know what your intentions are, but I want you to know I'm not interested in dating." She paid $425 for a bicycle at the Bike Out benefit during the live auction. Ravi was the auctioneer. When the bike was at $200, he said, "Come on, some of you pay that much for a pair of shoes." At $350, he threw in a date with me. At $400, he threw in two dates with me. She bid the highest and then gave the bike away to one of the Bike Out kids.

It was a classy move, but I'm not attracted to her.

She says, "That makes sense; you're busy. You're about to have a baby."

I say, "Yes, but even if I weren't, I still wouldn't be interested."

## WEEK 36, DAY 5

The woman I had a date with hates my guts. She told Ravi I have no filter and that I shouldn't treat people who are generous to my charity with so little sensitivity. I ask Ravi if he defended me. He says, "I said, 'That's the way Andrea is.' "

## WEEK 37

Approximately 47 people have told me, unsolicited, that I'm having a boy. Today, when I'm standing in line at the sandwich shop, the man behind me says, "I can feel that you're having a girl." He tells me he's psychic. He looks Tibetan.

I have my medical records from Kaiser in my filing cabinet. I could read through them and find out if I'm having a girl or a boy. I'm tempted, but I think not knowing will help me get through labor. It will give me something to look forward to.

I think my anxiety about circumcision is really my fear of having a boy. I'm terrified of boys; they're wild and smelly. I mistrust men. They think they know everything, like my dad, who was circumcised, and who said yesterday that the foreskin doesn't have any feeling.

I said, "There is no way you can know that."

"Well I know for a fact you don't need it," he said. Like I wanted to be talking to my dad about his penis.

## WEEK 37, DAY 2

Tomorrow is my last day of work. I am here late tonight, cleaning out my desk and clearing files from my computer. I write the new executive director a letter to officially welcome her. I wish her luck and good fortune with this little organization I care about so much. Writing the letter feels sad, but satisfying.

I write to Becca and say that I trust her 100 percent to keep Bike Out strong and that I will miss her. Overall I'm happy to be leaving. It's time. Bike Out has $70,000 in the bank. I have exceeded my goal.

## Week 37, day 3
I'm retired. I feel at ease.

I drink chicken soup and eat a big bowl of ice cream, even though Dana and the Tootsie Roll lady told me to lay off sugar. A half hour before my last appointment at the Birth Center, I ate a pack of Sugar Babies, and my pee test showed my urine was high in glucose. My body's not processing sugar as well as usual, or maybe I don't usually eat Sugar Babies before testing my urine. Either way, I was busted. Dana said that eating too much sugar bulks up the baby. Then she said my baby was nearing eight pounds.

Still, I have to have the ice cream.

Now Bean is sitting on my belly and we are both purring.

A lot of my friends have called to say congratulations and to check in on me. Even Kate called tonight. Maybe my dad is wrong about friends. Feels like he's wrong tonight.

## Week 37, day 4
I wake up feeling calm. I dreamt I met my donor. He was blonder and not as cute as I'd imagined, but not bad. He had a big nose. He was very nice. I asked him if he wanted to be part of the child's life. He said it was up to me.

He said I was a lot sexier than he thought I'd be.

## WEEK 37, DAY 5

My baby dropped. Not out. Certainly not out, but down. I went for a walk, and a mile from home I felt it. Suddenly, walking really hurt in my lower belly or my upper pubic area or somewhere around there. I needed a ride, but I made it home safely.

So now I'm at yoga, trying to stretch out. What a mistake. I can't do any of the postures, so I keep trying to do Child's Pose. My baby is squashed against the floor and the ligaments around my hips feel like they're ripping. Putting my head down also gives me acid reflux. Child's Pose is not for very pregnant women, but it's the best I can do.

When the teacher walks by, I whisper, "I'm a yoga under-achiever."

She says in a regular voice, "Get that out of your head. You are an inspiration. This is your practice." Yoga teachers make me laugh. They are always so positive about everything.

## WEEK 37, DAY 6

I'm enjoying my retirement.

I buy baby wipes today. Not for the baby. For me. I have hemorrhoids. This is to be expected during pregnancy.

## WEEK 37, DAY 7

I'll try anything to make this birth bearable, so today I go to a hypnobirthing therapist. I go in without much expectation except a little nagging feeling, like this better amount to something, at $75 an hour.

On the phone the therapist sounded hard and unfriendly. She had an accent, which I couldn't place, and I expected her to be blond, with sharp features.

I walk in and am surprised to see a round-faced, warm-eyed, dark, curly-haired woman. She's French. I like her immediately. She seems to like me. She says, "You look healthy and beautiful, Mommy."

She asks me general therapy questions, like what my family is like; am I close with my mom and dad; what was my path to pregnancy; what am I afraid of?

I speak easily and tell her I'm close with my family. I tell her that since coming out I've been working to get my mom back. I think I'm almost there, I say, but I still feel exiled from my home in Miami. I don't feel fully accepted there, so I've built a family of friends 3,000 miles away, here in Los Angeles.

I tell her I've spent many years dreaming of children with Kate, but that I'm alone now and sad that I don't have her to share this with. I say I'm most afraid of feeling vulnerable. I'm afraid of being totally open and out of control and alone.

She nods and listens carefully. "When you first came in here, I was very surprised by what you look like," she says. "You are extremely warm and your beauty is your vulnerability. I know you're afraid. That's natural. But when you act out of a place of fear, you don't allow people to help you."

"What do you mean?" I say, although what she says feels true.

"When you left me a message last night, you said you needed to come in after one, you needed to leave by four, and that I should call you back after ten. You didn't allow any flexibility and you didn't consider what I might need. To be honest, I was concerned about how I would handle you. Now I see you're just afraid.

"It's okay to be vulnerable. It's okay to say, 'I'm scared.' I want to help you let go of control, which is what you have to do to have an enjoyable birth. And to be a mom."

Everything she says makes sense and sounds so familiar, like I've learned this before. And not just about pregnancy, but about all my relationships. I've been acting out of fear.

I didn't have to tell the woman I went on a date with that I wasn't interested in dating her, *ever*. But I was compelled to tell the whole truth, to cut off the possibility of dating her entirely. I was scared to death of letting go of Kate.

My ex-therapist said I wasn't considering her when I told her I was leaving. I get it. Instead of saying, "I'm so scared," I just quit.

I haven't been able to admit my limitations and accept that I'm afraid. My fear ruined my relationship with Kate.

Four years ago, I did Outward Bound—23 days in the wilderness meant to push you past your breaking point. Outward Bound was created in 1941 to help merchant seamen build fortitude to survive war and shipwreck. I used it as training for Bike Out. But it became a lot more.

I was 30 years old and physically fit, or so I thought, and had always been able to trust my body. I was a cross-country runner in school and wouldn't slow down, even if I had to pee in my shorts to win. I could push my body to the extreme.

But Outward Bound was unrelenting: We woke up with the sun and hiked until dark. My backpack was so heavy I needed help getting it on my back. Once I had it on, I couldn't take it off and learned to fall into a tree or a hill to rest, with the pack still strapped to my shoulders.

I spent the last three days on the course with the worst diarrhea I had ever experienced. I felt wetness between my legs, in my sleeping bag, and thought I had lost control of my bowels. I was so tired I slept in it and didn't realize I'd gotten my period until morning.

When I got to the airport, Kate held me while I laughed hysterically. I didn't know why I was laughing; I just came undone.

I slept for ten days. I woke up hungry, and Kate took me to Chaya Venice. I ate a 16-ounce steak by myself (usually we shared), potatoes, a seaweed salad, and a giant Ben & Jerry's waffle cone for dessert. Kate said she'd never seen me eat like that. I think I was literally starving.

I went to the doctor to test for Giardia and dysentery, and because my fingers and toes had been tingling for two weeks, I told him I might have MS. I had done an MS bike-a-thon a few months before and had learned that MS presents itself in women my age and that tingling in the fingers and toes was one of the signs.

Before examining me he said, "You don't have MS."

"How do you know?"

"You just don't," he said.

I came home spitting mad. I told Kate about the arrogant, know-it-all doctor who didn't listen to me, and Kate said the same thing, "You don't have MS."

I didn't want MS, no way, but I thought for sure I had it. I could think of no other explanation for my body's failure. My body had limits, and that terrified me. I was so scared I couldn't admit it. Instead, I fought with Kate because she didn't agree with me.

Kate said, "Andrea, the reality is, you're just tired."

I tell my hypnotherapist about Outward Bound and the woman I had a date with, and even about my ex-therapist. She tells me to lie back and get comfortable. "I want you to quiet your mind and just feel. Note what you feel and then let it go. Just accept." She leads me through hypnosis, which is a process of deep relaxation—her strategy for handling whatever might come up during labor.

After the session, she says I went really deep. She is impressed. I think I might have fallen asleep.

## WEEK 38

Today we're having Thanksgiving dinner at my house: Ravi and his new boyfriend, Stephanie and her boyfriend, and me.

Last week I asked Ravi to burn a CD of my sperm donor's audio interview, which I had downloaded onto my computer. I e-mailed it to Ravi, and I thought he forgot about it. He walks in the door with two copies of 3342's interview on CDs. He made labels with pictures of sperm on them. This may be the nicest thing anyone's ever done for me. This and the fat-girl underwear. I hug Ravi for what seems like five minutes.

We meet at 12:30 to get the turkey started and spend the whole day together cooking and preparing for the baby. They help set up a small crib, called a co-sleeper, that attaches to the side of my bed, because I am still undecided about where the baby will sleep. We look through my shower gifts to assess what I still need and what to take back.

Ravi puts out fancy wine, Brie, olives, and cut-up pears, and we play poker with nickels and pennies. Every time I get a really good hand, I laugh uncontrollably. I know I have the worst poker face, and that makes me laugh harder. I win $3.45.

While we wait for the turkey, Steph makes stuffing and pumpkin pie, and I make sweet potatoes and a salad and cranberry sauce. Finally, the turkey's ready. When we sit down to eat, I think about Kate. I wish, just for a second, that she was sitting beside me, then I think: Stop. I'm having a wonderful night. We eat a ton, and I am thankful.

### Week 38, day 2
I'm cleaning the house like crazy. I throw out half-used hair gels and face cleansers and glasses I haven't worn in 12 years that are clogging up my bathroom and make way for diapers and baby products. Then I wash and fold all my baby clothes and place them neatly on a shelf I cleared in my closet. I pick out the outfit my baby will wear on his very first day outside the womb—the softest and most adorable cotton long-sleeved bodysuit ever made. There is a bear cub embroidered on the chest.

They say nesting is a sign the baby is on the way. I suppose being 38 weeks pregnant is also a sign.

## WEEK 38, DAY 3

Janet sent *The New Jewish Baby Book* to help with my decision about circumcision. It's not exactly an unbiased read, but it's a good complement to the anticircumcision propaganda I got at the Birth Center. It does say that according to the American Association of Pediatrics, there is no medical reason for circumcision, and it acknowledges that I'm not the only Jew struggling with whether or not to do it.

God asked Abraham to make a sacrifice and remove the foreskin, or *orlah*, a Hebrew word that means any barrier standing in the way of God. Rabbis have interpreted the act as a way of sanctifying sex. I like that.

Circumcision is a 4,000-year-old practice. It has been seen for centuries as a test of Jewish commitment. Sort of makes me feel guilty if I'm the one who breaks the chain.

Now I'm sitting at the breakfast table with a bowl of cereal and six jars of vitamins. I tested positive for Beta Strep, which is very common and no big deal except that one in 1,000 babies will contract it coming through the vagina, and it could lead to meningitis, which is fatal. So I'm taking a hard-core vitamin protocol twice a day, prescribed by the midwives, including four capsules of acidophilus, two capsules of Echinacea, two tablets of garlic, one vitamin C, and 15 drops of grapefruit seed extract. I also take my prenatal vitamin and drink a big glass of prune juice, which I had previously thought was the most sick-making thing in the world. No, the grapefruit seed extract tastes worse than chewing 100 grapefruit peels. But I am going to beat Beta Strep the natural way.

## Week 38, day 4

At noon, my mom and Bob come walking through the court-yard. I am standing in the doorway of their rented bungalow, right next door to mine.

My mom screams and covers her mouth and then rushes over to me. I've sent pictures, but she hasn't seen me since week 20. She is laughing and holding her hands to her face.

"My baby," she says. "I can't believe my baby's having a baby."

I have been holding on like someone who's waiting to die. Now the baby can come.

Today, I feel taken care of. My mom and Bob are living next door for the next two and a half months. By a stroke of amazing luck, my neighbors moved out a month ago, and the landlord agreed to give my mom a short-term lease. He's charging her enough for the privilege, but my mom can handle it. She and Bob are artists and can live and work anywhere.

My mom and Bob are keyed up with excitement. I take them to lunch, and we talk about my birth plan. Dana and Stephanie will come over when I begin labor, and Dana will drive me to the Birth Center while they follow. I tell Bob there's a lounge he can wait in. He says, "I've come all the way from Miami, and I don't even get to watch the birth."

My mom says, really loudly, "You can't watch the birth. That's Andrea's vagina."

I wonder if I'll miss being pregnant. This is impossible to imagine. I hate pregnancy so much, but soon no one will insist I'm having a boy. No one will ask when I'm due. No one will smile and ask to rub my belly. No one will carry my groceries to the car. No one will let me use the bathroom at the bank that's off-limits to customers. No one will get me a drink of water and tell me to stay seated. No one will say, "You look healthy and beautiful, Mommy."

Janet says, "Enjoy it now, girl; in a few weeks no one's going to even notice you. It'll all be about the baby."

## WEEK 38, DAY 6

I'm not going to circumcise. I heard on the radio today that George Washington and Thomas Jefferson owned slaves but struggled with it, morally. In the end, Washington and Jefferson bowed to cultural pressure. Some things are just wrong.

## WEEK 39

I wake up thinking that if by some miracle I have a girl, I want to have a baby-naming ceremony on New Year's Eve. I want to invite Robin's parents, who buried their daughter two years ago on New Year's Eve. I think they will appreciate this gesture. If not, it will be for Bob and me. Bob is Robin's uncle. He and my mom met at Robin's funeral. They have spent every day together since.

Bob lived in Robin's house for six months with the rest of the family while Robin was dying. Having Bob around keeps me connected to Robin. Being pregnant does too.

I take my mom to birth class, which really drags. I say, "Jen, we're pregnant; could you speed it up?" She smiles.

Jen talks about attachment parenting. Giving the kid everything it needs and breast-feeding for two to four years are the parenting practices they espouse at the Birth Center. My mom whispers, but I'm sure the whole class can hear, "What, the kid comes off the soccer field and takes a drink from your breast?"

Liz tells a story about a friend with a 2-year-old who tugs at his mom's shirt whenever he feels like it. That doesn't sound good to any of us. Jen tries to argue that it's important to meet the child's needs.

Jen talks about co-sleeping and my mom says to me during the break, "I don't agree with kids sleeping in the bed."

I pat her on the head and say, "I know you're the expert, but I might do things differently." Jen told us a few classes ago to always acknowledge that our moms are experts.

My mom says, "If you don't like my ideas, that's one thing, but don't patronize me."

"I'm sorry. I just don't know how I'm going to want to do things. Also, trust me, I don't agree with everything Jen says."

## WEEK 39, DAY 5

I take my mom to Kaiser today for my weekly appointment. Between Kaiser and the Birth Center, I'm getting way too much medical care. I don't see Dr. Martinez, because today's her day off. Instead, I get Nurse Jones, who shoves her fingers into my vagina like she's digging for a pickle at the bottom of the jar. I say, "That hurts!" and she just looks at me like, *Girl, this is nothing. If you can't handle this, you're in trouble.*

I'm not dilated, but Jones says I could have the baby any day. I ask if my fibroid's going to be a problem. Dr. Martinez already told me it wouldn't be, but I want a second opinion. She says no. I ask if she's sure, and she gives me another look.

"Will I know when I'm in labor?"

"Yes."

"I feel pain all the time. Maybe I'm in labor right now."

"You're not."

After my appointment my mom and I go to lunch and then shopping for pajamas. To make sure the jammies will be big enough and comfortable enough for postpartum, I try them on. As soon as we get into the dressing room, my mom says, loud enough for everyone in the other stalls to hear, "Your heinie. Your heinie is showing."

My butt isn't actually showing, but 25 years ago we heard

a mother say the same thing to her daughter in the Jordan Marsh dressing room.

I laugh, and my mom says, "I'm glad you haven't had the baby yet. I'm afraid the baby's going to come between us."

"As soon as I have the baby, you won't care about me anymore," I say.

## Week 40

Today's my due date. Okay, I'm ready.

I go to prenatal yoga to try to induce. I've heard of two cases where a woman's water broke after class on the way to the car. So I push myself. The woman beside me is so big she seems unnatural. She is so strong and can do every pose with ease. I try Downward Dog and tumble onto my side. I laugh.

Class is hard, and I am sweating and feeling good. Catherine, our teacher, ends the class by telling everyone to hug the big women up front. She's talking about me. "You may not see them without babies again," she says. The other big woman and I stand and get hugs. We stand back to back in the mirror. I'm even bigger than she is.

I tell Catherine this class has been one of the bright spots of my pregnancy.

I take my mom and Bob to the food co-op. My mom is as gung ho as I am about getting the provisions to take to the Birth Center when I go into labor. We get fruit-sweetened oatmeal cookies, organic apples, yogurt-covered pretzels, walnuts, dried cranberries, and almond butter. I'm packing food for an outdoor expedition.

A man in line says, "When are you due?"

"Today," I say.

"Oh, let me get out of your way," he says. This is fun.

My mom and I go to the Birth Center for an exam and my birth class. Dana does a vaginal exam to see if I'm dilated or effaced, which means the thinning out of the cervix. Dana is so gentle. She says, "I'm going to put my finger inside your vagina. Are you ready?"

"Can you tell where my fibroid is?"

"I think it's under your uterus. It may cause back pain, but don't worry, there is nothing in the way of the birth canal."

I'm 50 percent effaced and one centimeter dilated. I can't believe it. The kid is on the way.

Birth class is long but actually nice. Tonight is our final class, and I think all of us feel camaraderie. These women make me comfortable. They have opted for natural childbirth too. They are brave and cool.

Jen has us stand in a tight circle, all the pregnant bellies touching. Our partners stand behind us and our support people stand behind them. Stephanie has her arms around my waist, and she's patting my belly. My mom is behind her. Jen asks us to say a prayer or a wish for all of us. We go around slowly. I get hot and try to scoot out of the circle. Stephanie thinks I'm snuggling up. Stephanie says she wants all of us to remember a challenge we were able to achieve. My mom hopes the goddess will be with us. I say I hope we can connect with women from the beginning of time and for health. Yes, health is most important, Liz says.

## Week 40, day 2

Stephanie comes over to make breakfast. She is done with school for the semester and is ready for labor. She cuts up walnuts and blueberries and makes the best pancakes I've ever had. She brings the pancakes to me in bed, then she cleans everything up. I want a wife like Stephanie.

Liz from my birth class is a healing woman; she comes over to help induce labor with acupuncture. She is 38 weeks pregnant herself.

Liz puts needles in and I listen to my hypnobirthing tape. I am relaxed, but scared. My feet feel clammy.

Liz asks me if I have been masturbating, and I can feel that I'm blushing. I say yes. I have been more sexually turned on than I can remember feeling in years. Liz says orgasms help induce labor. She also suggests I squeeze my nipples.

"Whatever works," I say.

Stephanie and I go for a long walk on the beach. The day is beautiful, and I think anything is possible. I feel strong. We talk about Robin and how surreal and sad it is that she has been dead exactly two years. Her funeral was on New Year's Eve.

Janet, Stephanie, and I shared a hotel room a few miles from Robin's house and the funeral home. We bawled our eyes out that day, watching as the plain wooden casket was lowered into the ground with our friend inside. I thought from the sounds Janet was making that she was going to throw up. Janet said she had never seen me cry so hard.

After the service, we came back to our hotel room and ordered room service: a burger and fries for me, and pasta with portobello mushrooms for Stephanie, plus chicken fingers and a salad, ice cream on a brownie, and half a carafe of wine. Janet had been sleeping since 10 P.M. I tried to wake her, saying the ice cream was melting, but she was too tired.

We turned on *New Year's Rockin' Eve* with Dick Clark. Stephanie stood on the bed and danced hard to a Pink video. I'd never heard of Pink, but Steph knew all the words. "Welcome to Club 422!" she said. We were in room 422. We jumped on the bed like little kids and laughed hysterically.

For a second I thought of Robin and wondered if it was

okay for us to be having so much fun on the day of her funeral. It was ten seconds before midnight. Janet lifted her head. We counted down. We kissed on the lips and then went to sleep.

My mom makes beef ribs for dinner. Everything tastes so good. I have heard that in the last days it becomes harder to eat, because the baby leaves no room for the stomach. I eat three ribs, a baked potato, salad, and ice cream. Bob makes jokes about how big I am. I don't say anything, even though I hate it more than anything when a man comments on a woman's body, especially mine. But today I don't care. Say what you want; I am with child.

The four of us play Boggle, and we are competitive. I beat their asses, and it feels good.

## WEEK 40, DAY 4

Okay, where's my baby? It is Sunday and it's raining in Los Angeles and I don't know what to do with myself. Stephanie comes over and makes pancakes again. Andrea Stern calls and says she's been sitting home tapping her foot. Me too.

I am getting 15 phone calls a day asking if I've had my baby. Kate calls. The first friend I ever made in the world, when I was 3 years old, calls. An old college lover calls. My dad calls again. His message says, "Hang in there," and it makes me smile.

## WEEK 40, DAY 5

2:30 A.M.: I feel my first contraction. My uterus tightens around my baby and feels like a strong menstrual cramp. It hurts, but I'm excited. I lie in bed watching the clock for two hours while the contractions come every 20 to 30 minutes. My baby is coming.

9 A.M.: I haven't felt a contraction for a few hours. I call Dana. She tells me it's common for contractions to go away during

the day. She predicts they'll come back after sundown and that the baby will come either tonight or tomorrow night.

The thought of waiting two nights knocks my morale, but I know the baby is on the way. She tells me to rest as much as I can.

9:30 A.M.: Stephanie is here making pancakes. Pancakes are all I want. Then we go for a very slow walk to the beach. Today is one of those days, after a big rain, that make Los Angeles a beautiful place to live. The sky looks squeegeed clean and bright blue and Malibu and the San Gabriel Mountains are clear and visible from the beach.

I feel three contractions as we walk. Walking is supposed to bring on labor.

3:30 P.M.: I lie down to nap.

3:45 P.M.: A strong contraction cinches my lower back and belly. It feels like I have to pee and poo.

4:02 P.M.: A contraction lasts for one minute and 20 seconds. Contractions continue and come five minutes, ten minutes, eight minutes apart. Another contraction lasts two minutes. Pain shoots down my thighs. Makes me sweat.

5:00 P.M.: Liz comes over to give me an acupuncture treatment. Instead, she presses certain points to strengthen labor—the inside of the calf four fingers above the ankle, between the thumb and finger, and the highest points on the shoulder. She has Stephanie massage my feet and hands. My mom comes in.

The stained-glass lamp in my bedroom casts an orange light, and I feel like I'm in the red tent, where women went in biblical times to have babies and have their period. The women took care of each other in the tent. Beautiful women are sitting around my bed, taking care of me, waiting for my baby to come.

My mom makes a turkey for dinner. I eat two slices of apple with honey. I have no appetite. I go back to my room while everyone finishes dinner. I do yoga poses, or some variation, during contractions. I feel like a cat stretching my back and legs. This seems to help. I yell out when the contractions start and finish. Stephanie times them and writes them down.

8:15 p.m.: I call Dana. I am nervous suddenly. I say, "I think the baby's coming. My contractions are strong and long."

She says long contractions usually indicate early labor. I trust her, but I also think I have a high tolerance for physical pain and fear the baby is closer than we think. Dana says to call her in a couple of hours. She's going to the gym.

I lie down and listen to my hypnobirthing tape. The tape relaxes me. Stephanie records my contractions during the tape: six minutes, nine minutes, six, six, four, seven, five, six, three minutes apart.

10:00 p.m.: I call Dana and ask her to come over. I need her. She asks for directions and I can barely think or speak. I hand the phone to Stephanie, and Dana is on her way.

10:30 p.m.: Dana arrives. My mom feeds her dinner, and she has tea while I am having contractions. Finally, she does a vaginal exam. I am 80 percent effaced and four centimeters dilated. I am in active labor.

She says, "I'm surprised you're so calm."

I say, "I'm surprised you're so calm."

11:30 p.m.: Dana drives me to the Birth Center, while Stephanie and my mom and Bob follow. I have six contractions in the car. It is difficult in the car; I can't stretch or bend. I tell Dana that right now I am not sad to be doing this without a partner. She tells me her labor was very lonely, because she expected her husband to help, but he couldn't. This is a solo expedition, and I am fine with that.

### Week 40, day 6

Midnight: The Birth Center is quiet and dark, but soon we make it bustle. I take a shower for 45 minutes, feeling the hot water beat on my back.

12:45 A.M.: I feel like I have to take a huge shit during every contraction, which seems to make them hurt even worse. I lean over in the shower and Dana gives me an enema. A dark brown blob of slime falls out of my body and onto the bathroom floor. Dana says it's probably the mucus plug and wipes it up with toilet paper. The mucus plug blocks the uterus, protecting the fetus from the outside world, and it has to come out before the baby. She smells it to make sure. It is the mucus plug. I am in awe of Dana.

The enema cleans me out but does nothing to relieve the pressure against my colon. The sensation of having to shit is overwhelming.

1:30 A.M.: I am in the birthing room, naked on the bed. I press my head against the bed with my ass in the air. I think for a second about the view everyone's getting. No one seems to care.

2:00 A.M.: Dana tests me, and I am seven centimeters dilated. I ask her to fill the birthing tub. I think the tub is the final frontier—where I will have my baby.

2:20 A.M.: The tub is warm and soothing and helps between

contractions. The contractions seem to slow down, but they are more intense when they come. I ask Dana how much longer. She says, "Probably 7 A.M."

"What? Five more hours? No!" My eyes well up. I say I might throw up and she holds a metal pan under my chin.

She says, "We never know."

4:10 A.M.: I am nine centimeters, pruned and exhausted. I am a caged rat. Stephanie and Dana are politely looking on. They look very tired. My mom is sitting quietly in the corner. She is handling this well. Dana periodically adds warm water to the tub.

The light is dim in the birth room. It is quiet outside. There is no sound except Diana Ross and the Supremes. "Stop in the Name of Love" is playing low. Stephanie thought music would help. The music does, strangely, comfort me, but it also feels like we're at a freaky party where everyone's doing a lot of drugs and nobody's having fun.

"This is so somber," I say.

"You're doing great," Dana says.

"I'm not interested in being great at this," I say. I just want the baby out.

4:45 A.M.: A contraction hurts worse than anything I have ever felt. My whole body is gripped by it. When it subsides, I tell Dana I feel like pushing. Dana checks my dilation. "It's not time to push," she says. "You're still nine centimeters."

"Please let me push."

She says, "If you push now, the cervix will swell and slow you down. Blow air out through your mouth for five contractions." The lip of my cervix is holding on.

I am demoralized. I want to stop. I look down at my huge belly and see that I've made no progress. Dana doesn't know what she's talking about.

I blow through five contractions, which takes a half hour. Blowing makes it impossible to push. I ask to be checked again.

5:15 A.M.: "Five more," Dana says.

"FUCK!"

Dana says, "Andrea, if you fight, the contractions hurt more." Her tone is strict.

I say, "They hurt anyway, Dana."

But I try not to fight. "Hurry, my baby, we can do this. Hurry, my baby, we can do this."

I want to cry. I wish I could cry. But I'm too tired or too vulnerable. I fall asleep in the tub twice between contractions. Falling into the water wakes me. I have never been this tired. Never felt such sustained physical pain. Hours have passed, and what started as barely bearable continues to get worse.

6:00 A.M.: Dana checks again. "Nine," she says. I hate Dana.

She asks if I want her to break my water. I say, "Please do whatever you can to speed this up. She reaches in with what looks like a crochet hook. I don't care. I open my legs. I want her to pull the baby out.

My bag is broken. Dana puts her fingers inside to manually push back the lip of my cervix so that the baby's head can get through. After 15 hours, it's time to push.

6:10 A.M.: I'm bad at pushing. I feel like a failure. "Please, my baby, hurry, my baby."

Dana says, "Push into the pain."

6:30 A.M.: I feel my hips splitting. Holy shit, my hipbones are ripping apart. Dana says this is good. Everything terrible is good to Dana.

7:15 A.M.: I tell Dana I'm done. I want to go to the hospital. She says if we go to the hospital now I won't get the epidural for an hour and a half and I will have had the baby by then. She says, "When you're this desperate, it's almost over." I knew she would say that.

7:28 A.M.: "Push," Dana says.

I can't push. I'm afraid shit will come out in the water. I'm afraid of what else might come out. What if the baby's ugly or deformed, or what if the baby's dead?

I look up and notice Stephanie taking my picture, as she's been doing all night. "Stop," I say. "I'm really suffering. Please get out. Everybody."

Stephanie and my mom leave quickly.

7:33 A.M.: I get out of the tub and pace the room, crazed and hysterical. I don't know what to do, but my legs can't hold me. Dana helps me get on the bed. I'm leaning back in the position women have babies in on TV. Dana says this is a good position. She says my pushes are excellent. She is so encouraging. Right now I need it. "I can feel the head," Dana says. "I feel the baby's hair. Push hard."

7:41 A.M.: "I *see* your baby's head." She holds up a mirror and I see the head when I push. Then the head retreats.

7:46 A.M.: "Little pushes now. Pant between pushes." I do what she says. We rehearsed pushing and panting. Dana is guiding my baby's head slowly to stretch my perineum. This is called the *ring of fire*.

7:52 A.M.: "Okay, push hard." I moan like a walrus. The baby's head is out.

"Pull," I say. The shoulders are stuck.

7:59 A.M.: "Push." My vagina tears open to my ass, but I don't care. I push, and in one slick motion, my baby is born.

Dana puts the baby on my chest. The cord is still attached inside and pulls on my vagina. I'm shaking. The baby's eyes are wide open and looking at me. The eyes are dark gray and so beautiful. The nose is squashed.

I can't believe it's out. I have a baby. I cry. The baby cries.

"Is it a boy or a girl?"

"Look," Dana says. I look.

It's a girl.

# Postpartum

## ONE DAY

My big baby (8 pounds, 14 ounces) is born and I name her Natasha Rain Askowitz. Natasha, because I think it's a beautiful name, and Rain, because we need rain. Her Hebrew name is Ari, a boy's name, I have been told, but I don't care. Ari means lion and I have a special affection for lions. And it starts with an A, like Albert, the name of my grandpa—my number one—who died when I was ten weeks pregnant. It's Jewish tradition to name a child after a late loved one by using the first letter of their name. I feel proud to have done my part.

Already everyone calls her Tashi, except my mom, who calls her Tasha.

I am so tired, but while my baby takes her first nap, curled up on her side on the bed where she was born, I call my dad, my brother, my grandma, and Janet, who says I have the best breasts for breast-feeding: small with big nipples. I think she might be right.

When Dana gives her her first bath, Tashi cries hard. I watch and trust that she's okay. I'm not scared like I was the time Kate and I baby-sat for my niece Rachel when she was less than a year old. Rachel cried for more than an hour. Kate and I sang to her and held her and rocked her, but we couldn't soothe her. I thought there was something terribly wrong and called my mom, who ended up singing to her over the phone. Kate said, "How can you be so ridiculous? Babies cry. What kind of mom will you be?" But I didn't know Rachel the way I know Tashi, even though she's only three hours old.

At noon, the receptionist at the Birth Center brings me the phone. It's Kate. She had woken up several times in the night: at midnight, when I first arrived at the Birth Center, at 2, when I got into the tub, and at 6, when Dana broke my bag of water and it was time to push. The receptionist told me Kate had left a message at 8, a minute after my baby was born. Kate was with me in some way during the night. She's not surprised I had a girl.

We stay at the Birth Center until 5 P.M., and then Stephanie drives us home. When I carry Tashi into the house, I say, "This is where we live." My heart has never felt bigger. From now on, I will share my home.

Kate and Ravi come over. Andrea Stern brings Chinese food, and Stephanie bakes my favorite kind of cake from a mix: yellow cake with chocolate frosting. She puts a zero candle on top and we all sing "Happy Birthday" to the baby.

I get into bed with Tashi and nurse, as I've been doing all day. Kate stays to watch. Tashi falls asleep, and I gently put her down on the bed beside me and fall asleep also. Kate gets into bed with us.

Two days

I spend most of Tashi's first night staring at her while she sleeps. Dana told me to wake her every three hours to nurse, because she'd be worn out from labor. But waking her doesn't seem right. Tashi sleeps for seven hours straight.

I love having Kate there all night, but what feels unbelievable is that I don't need her. I'm not desperate, and I'm not scared, as I had feared. I am simply in awe.

At noon Stephanie takes Tashi and me to the pediatrician. I leave the house with my hands full: Tashi wrapped in a thin blanket, plus my donut pad—the toilet seat–like sponge to sit on so my butt and vagina will heal. I don't know which hurts worse, the stitches on my perineum or the hemorrhoids the size of grapes. Janet calls and says, "Doesn't it feel like you shat your ass inside out?"

Tashi looks a little yellow, so the pediatrician takes blood from her heel. Tashi cries. When he goes to take blood from the other heel, Stephanie says, "Tashi, this is your chance to say, 'What do you think, I was born yesterday?'"

When I take off her diaper for the exam, she pees on her little blanket. I don't have a spare. I don't even have a spare diaper. I carry Tashi, with no clothes on, into the cool December afternoon, and the receptionist chases after us. She wraps Tashi in a big hospital blanket before letting us go home.

Kate surprises us and comes over again, and I am happy. She takes a bath, and I go next door to tell my mom to make extra spaghetti for dinner. Bob says, "What's Kate doing in the bath?"

"Relaxing," I say. It is none of his business. Kate's not a regular friend. She's my family. She can take a bath in the house we lived in together if she wants to.

## ONE WEEK

Tony and Lisa and my nieces and my dad and Elsa are in town to meet the baby. I am still in pajamas, and my boobs are showing all the time because it's a constant feeding. Normally I wouldn't care, and especially now, because my boobs look better than they've ever looked. And I'm proud to be breast-feeding and think it's the most natural function on earth. But right now I wish I had a little more energy to rein them in.

Tashi can lift her head. Everyone is so impressed.

## TWO WEEKS

Friends have been coming over to see us. I am open to friends again. My mom has everyone wash his or her hands before touching the baby. When Dave held Tashi without putting a burp cloth over his shoulder, my mom threw a fit. I thought burp cloths were used to protect the person holding the baby from unwanted spit-up on the shoulder. But my mom thinks burp cloths are used to protect the baby from dangerous mi-crobes on somebody's shirt. I told my mom Tashi could han-dle it, even if she's only two weeks old.

My mom is a godsend. She provides all the meals and keeps the house clean and helps me be a mother. Yesterday at 10 A.M., I knocked on my mom and Bob's door. They rushed out and welcomed Tashi like it was the first time they'd seen her. My mom said, "Oh, today's the day. Tasha's peaked. She has reached her all-time cutest."

Today I knock again at 10 A.M. They rush out. My mom says, "Today's the day. Tasha's peaked."

Every day, I get about an hour and a half to myself before Tashi needs to nurse again.

I have a crush like no other I've ever experienced. It's one-sided, pure, and egoless, having nothing to do with the love I'm getting in return, since I'm not getting any love in return. Just blank stares that are so intoxicating. And every day my love grows, unbidden, even when feeling more seems impossible.

### Three weeks

Tashi seems to have discovered what crying is for. My mom bounced her for hours last night, but she didn't stop crying until she fell asleep at midnight.

Years ago, Kate and I were hanging out listening to the radio. A familiar song was on, but I never knew which group played what song, which always embarrassed me. I asked Kate who was playing. She said, "You don't know?"

I cried. I was surprised and ashamed by it, but there were tears coming out of my eyes and I couldn't fight them.

Kate had cried many times about all sorts of things. She'd cry hard before a stressful interview and then perform like a champ, like Holly Hunter in the '80s movie *Broadcast News*. She'd come home from work exhausted and cry for apparently no reason, then regroup and feel better. Kate made crying look easy and natural.

Kate hugged me. She laughed a little, but not in a condescending way, more in a way that made me feel like it was okay. "It's The Grateful Dead, 'Uncle John's Band.' "

I want to let Tashi know, right from the beginning, that it's okay to cry.

### Four weeks

Tashi had a good, two-hour nursing session at 6 P.M. Then again at 10 P.M. And again at 3 A.M.

At the first light of day I call Janet to ask how long Tashi should nurse. "The rule of thumb," she says, "about fifteen minutes on each breast."

"Oh, so two hours is too long?"

"You gotta stop the grazing," she says.

## EIGHT WEEKS

When people meet Tashi, they say she has a mellow vibe. They don't see her at night when she's nursing like a spaz, flopping her head around, gunning for the nipple and missing. When that happens, I think maybe she's blind.

## 12 WEEKS

My mom and Bob left six days ago, and I didn't fall apart. I was sure I would, but this is what Tashi has taught me: that fantasies are always better and fears are always worse than reality.

I'll admit that doing anything, even buttering a piece of toast, is nearly impossible by myself because I am always holding the baby. But no big deal; I just eat a lot of toast without butter.

I invite the women from my birth class and their babies over for lunch. I want to share birth stories and stories about motherhood. For all seven of us, this is our first child. Liz comes early to help me prepare lunch. With Judah asleep in a sling across her chest, she cuts up fruit. I breast-feed Tashi and put out bagels and spreads. I'm slowly learning to double-task while breast-feeding. Liz asks me if I think we'll have anything in common with the other moms, but soon everyone comes with their newborns, and we talk for hours.

We decide to take turns hosting a lunch once a week. I call us the Breast-feeding Club. I tell Stephanie and she says, "You guys are the Nipple Ring."

**16** WEEKS

Dear Tashi,

We are with our friends today at the Nipple Ring. April is hosting and thought it would be a cool idea to write our kids a letter to tell you what life is like with you. You are falling asleep in my lap right now. You are an angel, dear one. You look long and strong and more beautiful than anything I have ever seen.

The Nora Jones CD *Come Away with Me* is playing. I wonder if we will still be listening to CDs when you are old enough to read this. Definitely not. When I was a kid, we listened to records, then 8-track tapes, then cassette tapes, and now CDs. Technology moves quickly.

The CD reminds me of your first three or four weeks. Every night, we danced to Nora Jones. I was too tired to change the CD. Hearing it today makes me miss those times when you were little.

I understand why women want more children. This time is so sweet and tender. I don't want it to end, although I also want to say that each day gets more fun.

Yesterday in yoga you lay on your blanket, wide-eyed, smiling, making circles with your mouth and *ooooohh* sounds with your deep, squeaky voice. Apparently, you have a lot to say. I can hardly do yoga when you're that cute.

A beautiful thing happened earlier today at the Nipple Ring. The other mommies were going on about which of their sons would be your boyfriend and how you're so lucky because you'll be able to take your pick, and then one of the moms said, "Wouldn't it be funny if Tashi is like her mother, and she doesn't want any of our boys?"

And then April said, "Or what if our boys are gay and aren't interested in Tashi?"

That was a big moment for all of us: mothers acknowledging the possibility that their sons might be gay. I think we're doing a good thing by hangin' in the ring.

I love you, my baby. I want you to know that, always.

Love, Mom

## 20 WEEKS

When do I start counting Tashi's age in months? Today she is 20 weeks old. She is four and a half months old, but no one says that.

Tashi's 12-week doctor's appointment came and went without her getting her vaccinations. None of the babies in the Nipple Ring have gotten shots, and some are never getting any. These women think the government is controlled by profit-hungry drug companies and that the vaccines aren't proven to be safe. Janet's kids started their shots at three months, on the conventional schedule, and so did my nieces.

The Nipple Ring circulated a book that suggests a link between autism and vaccines. Even though I'd maxed out on pregnancy and motherhood books in my first trimester, I borrowed *What Your Doctor May Not Tell You About Vaccinations*.

Today I wish I had someone to share this huge responsibility, someone better at researching to gather and distill this kind of information. Of course, I'm thinking about Kate, who is brilliant in this way. I wonder if she would actually do this research, and I do it myself.

The book, clearly biased against vaccines, does not persuade me that there's a clear link to autism or any diseases. I decide that the risk of not vaccinating is greater than the risk of vaccinating.

I'm tired and down. Tashi is grumpy too. She's crying more than usual and is eating and pooping and eating and pooping and wants to be held constantly. I wonder if Tashi can sense my moods. Does she mirror me? Sometimes she seems to, and then I think, no, she's having her own moods. I ate cereal this morning, and the cow's milk, filtered through my breasts, is probably what's upsetting her, more than my mood. Dana says it takes a half hour for whatever I eat to show up in my milk. I think Tashi's lactose intolerant.

I wonder if I mirror Tashi. I read a study that showed that instead of babies copying the faces of their parents, it's the other way around. When babies smile and coo, their parents smile and coo. I want to be careful to keep my emotions separate from Tashi's.

### Five months

I take Tashi to the doctor for her first round of shots; she handles them better than I do.

We're in Miami because I finally got it together to have a baby-naming ceremony. This Jewish ritual for girls usually happens around one month, but I gave myself leeway since I'm a single mom. I invited friends and family and extended family and asked Stephanie to be Tashi's godmother and to facilitate the ceremony, which she did yesterday in a big circle in my mom's yard.

Stephanie and I talked for hours about what it all means: godmotherhood, God, motherhood, Judaism, lesbianism, and publicly naming a baby. At the ceremony, Stephanie said that I, as her lifelong friend, have helped shape who she has become. "It's the job of the people in Natasha's life to help shape who she'll become," she said. "We have to give her the freedom to interpret traditions in her own way, to respect differences, and especially to question."

Questioning is the Jewish custom I want Tashi to inherit. Through questioning comes social consciousness. I want her to think for herself and to question convention, because she might need to with a lesbian, single mom.

Kate flew in from Los Angeles and made a speech during the ceremony. She told everyone how for years I had been trying to whip her into shape to be my co-mom. That every time we'd see kids playing in a park, I'd say, "Come on Kate, get ready." She said she understands now why it was so important for me to have a baby. "Andrea is complete," she said. "She was born for this role."

Kate has come home with me several times over the years, but she was never introduced as my lover. Good for her for speaking so easily about our time together. Good for all of us.

Some of the people who were there I'd grown up with but hadn't seen since my grandpa's funeral or even since I was a kid. I think, by now, they know I'm a lesbian, but not one of them asked me how Tashi came to be. I thought about telling them, but this was a celebration of Tashi, not an explanation of me.

In my immediate family, my lesbianism doesn't seem to matter anymore. I am no longer a lesbian first. Now I'm a mom.

The single, black-sheep, hippie kid who lives in California is now a legitimate Askowitz family member. My status is equal to my brother's, because I have my own family. Now I have a vote on where we go out to dinner. And I'll probably get my own room on family vacations.

The baby seems to have erased years of hurt and rejection, and I finally feel reunited. But I wonder if my family has really changed. I wonder if my exile was self-imposed.

## Six months

I wake up before Tashi, which is a miracle. Tashi is sleeping peacefully between her baby bumpers—two firm triangular pillows wedged on either side of her to keep her from rolling—so I sneak out of bed to make breakfast. Breast-feeding makes me so hungry. I cut up tomatoes, onions, and peppers and, for the first time since having Tashi, I sit down at the table alone and eat a giant omelet.

The last time we saw Robin, about four weeks before she died, Janet and I met at a diner. We shared an omelet and waffles, and Janet said, "Can you imagine not being able to eat?" Robin hadn't eaten since her colon surgery, three weeks before. We thought she might never enjoy food again.

Janet had called from her cell phone, as we were instructed, to see if Robin was up for our visit. She gave us the okay to come over. I worried the two of us would overwhelm her, but we had been a threesome ever since we skipped school and went to the beach together 17 years ago.

We were greeted at the door by Robin's dad and led toward the living room. Robin was coming down the stairs from her bedroom. She walked slowly. She looked ghostly, but elegant. She said, "I don't feel like sitting in my room anymore."

Janet rushed up to greet her, and I was impressed. Janet seemed to know what to do. I stood at the bottom of the stairs and watched and waited.

We hugged, finally. Robin was stiff. Maybe she was worried about how her body would feel to me. Maybe she was worried about the tubes taped and plugged into her: two on her shoulder for pain control and nutrients and two on her stomach to act like a colon and intestines. I was careful.

She sat down on the couch. I sat on the floor in front of

her. I sat up on my knees like I was about to polish her nails. Robin said: "Please, not so close."

Oh God, I made her feel like a sick person. I felt big and clumsy, like I might break something. She asked me to sit on the other couch. I did, but I wanted to be closer. I wanted to be much closer.

Robin asked what was going on with us, and I chattered about a guy I had met who I thought would make a perfect sperm donor. I was distracted by a beeping sound. Janet said she thought she heard a cell phone ring.

Robin said, "It's my pain medicine." The bag attached to her shoulder gave her a constant flow. If it wasn't enough, she'd conspicuously unzip the bag, reach in with her thin finger, and administer an extra dose. "I have to wait ten minutes between doses, or it'll beep."

I was shaken, but I continued explaining to my straight, married friends what I wanted in a sperm donor. "Someone smart, of course, and cute, but someone who would be okay not having any parental rights." Robin's pain medicine beeped again.

Robin said, "It would be so hard to have a baby alone." She'd told me this before, but this time it sounded less like a rebuke and more like concern.

Robin lifted her shirt and, without emotion, said: "Look at what has become of my life." We saw the tubes and bandages and a scar going down from her belly button. Her breasts were smaller than they used to be.

"How are you feeling?" Janet said.

"I'm okay right now," she said. This sounded familiar. So many times in high school, after we had stayed up all night studying or talking, I'd be wasted the next day and I'd complain about it. But Robin never said she was tired. If I asked, she'd say: "I'm okay right now."

Was this acceptance, or denial?

"It took me two hours to get ready for you guys," Robin said. That morning she had taken an upper through one of her IVs so she wouldn't be spacy from the pain medication—morphine. For an hour she had to pinch the tube leading to the colostomy bag or the drug would have gone right through her without being digested.

"I'm done with treatment from Sloan-Kettering," she said. "The chemo isn't working."

This we knew. We didn't say anything. Robin said, "My dad is researching alternatives. I didn't get enough time before going to experimental treatments." It had only been five months since her daughter was born and they found the cancer.

We talked about his research; how it's possible to get drugs from other countries that aren't FDA approved, but that aren't well tested either.

"If anyone can get them, your dad can," Janet said.

It all seemed futile and so scary. "Do you want to try experimental treatments?" I asked.

Robin said, "If I don't..." She looked at me and then Janet. Her eyes looked way too big in her shrinking face. They welled up with tears, but she didn't cry. I moved closer and Janet, who was already on the couch with Robin, rubbed her outstretched foot. Janet repeatedly stroked Robin's foot.

Robin said, "Enough."

And that was all that was said about the possibility of our friend dying.

I finish eating, and before Tashi wakes up I call Janet. I ask, "Do you still have that necklace with the _J_ on it?"

Janet laughs a little. She knows what I'm talking about.

One Sunday morning, when we were about 16, the three of us were walking through a giant, crowded, flea market. I was haggling for a pair of jeans when I heard Janet scream. I turned around and saw Janet holding her neck. Some guy had grabbed her necklace from behind. Then Robin jumped on his back. She held on to his dirty white T-shirt, like she was riding a bull, until he flung her to the ground and ran away.

I laugh. "I can't believe Robin jumped that guy."

## SEVEN MONTHS

Today I'm hosting the Nipple Ring. We haven't missed a single Wednesday since we started. I think, for all of us, Wednesday is the best day of the week. We eat well and breast-feed until late in the evening, talking about diapers, breast engorgement, leaking, peeing, nipple blisters, co-sleeping, cribs, strollers, car seats, and sex.

It's 6 P.M., and April, Liz, Rana (a new Ring member), and I are eating another round of bagels and egg salad: my gourmet contribution to the ring. The women don't complain. We love all food. April opens a bottle of wine, and we settle in for another couple of hours. Our babies are falling asleep in our laps.

Liz says, "I haven't had sex since Judah was born."

"I've read that breast-feeding takes away your libido," Rana says.

"I've given two blow jobs, that's it," April says. "But I don't want no penis inside me."

"I don't either," Liz says. "I feel so in love with David, but I'm sucked dry. And I'm afraid of how it will feel down there."

I'm amazed. I thought I was the only one not getting any. But my lot is really not so different from my married friends'.

## EIGHT MONTHS

I sit down with Tashi on the floor of her room and read *Where the Wild Things Are.* I get to the roaring of their terrible roars and the gnashing of their terrible teeth and remember when Kate and I worked on a children's book together, before we became lovers. I had the idea, but Kate had the poetry. To get me to hear the rhythm, she'd say, " 'They roared their terrible roars and gnashed their terrible teeth.' "

Kate and I fought during the production of that book. She wanted an outline, and I wanted to trust where the writing would take us. She said, "Andrea, you can't do everything your way."

Now I get it.

When Robin said, "Andrea always wants to get her way," she meant that I didn't ask her what she wanted. I'd ask to sit outside at a restaurant, when maybe she wanted to sit inside. I'd insist on pizza for lunch, when maybe she wanted sandwiches. I'd make her come to my house instead of going to hers, because I didn't like driving.

Maybe I didn't ask Robin how she was feeling. I certainly didn't ask Kate.

With Tashi I have no choice. I have to consider her first. Tashi makes me better.

### NINE MONTHS

Tashi has been outside the womb as long as she was inside. And now she's crawling like a regular baby. And she has one tooth. And I swear she's talking, pointing her finger at everything, all day long, saying, "What's that?" She skipped single words and went straight to full sentences. She can also roll her tongue like she's practicing her Spanish *rr*. It's the craziest, most beautiful sound.

I wonder if Tashi will be girly or butch. Will she want to be a boy? I did. My grandfather told Tony and me that if we could kiss our elbows, I'd turn into a boy and he'd turn into a girl.

I was probably six years old, and Tony was eight. We tried so hard, but it was impossible. Maybe Tashi will do more than try to kiss her elbow and really want to be a boy, like some of the Bike Out youth who feel they were born into the wrong gender. How will I handle that? Will I be able to accept my baby girl as a boy?

My friends have been asking me if I think she'll be gay. I welcome this question as I welcome all questions. I think parents should consider the possibility, and it gives me a chance to ask if they think their child will be gay.

I don't have a hope for her either way. I want only that she feels secure and that she finds love. I hope that, with a lesbian mother, she'll feel free to be whoever she is and love whoever she loves.

I wonder what her rebellion will look like. I predict that the next boundary-pushing gesture, after tattoos have gone out of style, will be face implants, like Spock ears or pointy chins or fangs. Will I still think she's the most beautiful child in the world if she has fangs?

TEN MONTHS

I spend the day in the Santa Monica Mountains with Stephanie and the Lesbian Campers. Tashi is strapped to my body in a sling as we hike the same path I hiked along when I was pregnant and afraid of rattlesnakes. I'm not afraid anymore.

When I was pregnant, I was sure that I had entered a long, dark period of isolation. That it would be years before I had an adult conversation about something other than diapers. That romantic love was so many years away I'd be old and ugly by that time, and if I was spared, at least I would no longer be interested. I was afraid to leave my career and, along with it, my identity. I felt trapped. And mine was a premeditated pregnancy in the first degree. I had brought it on myself. I remember telling Kate that I'd ruined my life.

"What life?" she said.

She was right. What did I have to lose?

Here I am, hiking the same trail as before. Only this time I'm carrying a heavier load. I can hang out with the lesbians if I want to, and my best friend is still my best friend. Only better. And our conversations go beyond diapers, way beyond. We talk about stuff I never imagined.

"I want Tashi to just know about her donor from the very beginning," I say. "I want it to be natural and normal."

"Maybe you should wait until she's old enough to understand," Steph says.

"When is that?"

"Six, or so."

"Then it will feel like some serious, bizarre thing."

"It is serious," Stephanie says.

"I don't want her to feel like a freak. Or like she's missing out. Maybe I'll get her to say it like: 'How big is Tashi? So big?' I'll say, 'Who's Tashi's donor? 3342.' "

Stephanie stops walking. Tashi is waking up; her head bobs from side to side. Stephanie looks at me funny. "Okay, maybe that's weird," I say.

## 11 MONTHS

I get a letter in the mail from Kate. Letters from Kate are always a gift. They are the best of Kate—smart, fun, adorable handwriting, cartoon doodles, poetry, and Kate's huge, loving heart. I have saved every one of them. I expect this one to be a thank-you for helping move her mother into an assisted-living facility because of Alzheimer's. And in a way it is.

We've been back a few days from Chicago and the most intense week Kate and I have ever spent together. We have an agreement that if anything this big comes up we will be there for each other, no matter what is going on in our relationship.

Kate supported me when Robin was sick. I will support Kate while her mother is sick.

We went to clean out Kate's mother's house: her desk, closets, and kitchen drawers. While Tashi slept, we boxed up the life of a sober ex-nun. We sifted through the Christmas ornaments Kate had been decorating the tree with since she was a little girl. I found a dove her mom bought with my name on it. I found the one with the picture of Kate, Coffee Bean, and me.

We read through old letters, deciding which to recycle and which to file away. We found a piece of paper dated September 4, 1969, two years before Kate was born, listing reasons to stay and reasons to leave the convent. First on the list to leave was her desire to have children.

While I was pulling an old rug to the curb, Kate came outside and held on to me. She cried into my shoulder. She begged me to come back to her. I trusted Kate more than I trusted myself, on matters of the heart, and I was so used to Kate being sure we were not right together. This switch scared the shit out of me. Did she mean it? I kissed her head over and over and said, "My Honey, I know you're sad. You want your mom, not me."

Kate writes: "If I am such a sunny angel, like you say I am, how could you ever let me go?"

I don't know. I don't know if it's possible to love someone so deeply and for so long, and to have her in my heart and to dream of building a family together, and then to let her go. But I owe it to myself and to Kate and especially to Tashi to try.

ONE YEAR
Natasha Rain Askowitz is one today. She is the most beautiful child I have ever seen. Just like in the dream I had before I peed on my pregnancy stick: She has brown curly hair and

looks like a boy, but she's a girl. She wears white terry-cloth footy pajamas and is tall for her age.

She's happy and zany, in her little way, throwing her arms up when I say, "Hip-hip-hooray!" She sucks her thumb with her chubby palm open so that her fingers go into her eyes. Stephanie says some people are a good hang no matter what their age. Tashi's a good hang, she says.

At one, Tashi is finally sleeping in her crib. My mom and Janet thought I was a hippie freak letting her sleep in bed with me. And I don't know how I functioned, since I woke up every three hours, all night, to nurse. Now we're down to one middle-of-the-night feeding. Janet's daughter was sleeping through the night at seven weeks. Still, I couldn't imagine doing it any other way.

I planned to breast-feed for a year, and I feel proud that I've made it. Breast-feeding has been mostly joyful since the blisters healed. Now Tashi is slowly weaning. I know I'll miss it, but it's time to get my body back for good. I've started cutting back on daytime feedings by distracting her and feeding her something else, which is a new challenge for me, but Tashi seems to like food in any form. And she has the perfect baby body to show for it. She looks just like Eliot Fox-Askowitz, the pudgy little baby in the picture Kate gave me, only she's still too young for roller skates.

My dad asks me if being a mom is harder than I thought it would be, and again I realize that my fears were far worse than the reality. I say, "It's more work, but it's easier." The physical tasks are backbreaking: changing her diaper on the floor of a public bathroom when there's no changing table, carrying her in the car seat when she's fallen asleep, getting her into pajamas when she wriggles to get away. But emotionally, being a mom is easier than I expected. I think I'm even good at it.

The moment Tashi was born, I was different. I was calm and confident and completely content—the best me I've ever been. My anxiety faded, and for the first time that I can remember, I wasn't hoping for an imaginary future when life would be better. I was happy right where I was. I was proud of my decision to have a baby alone and felt strong and bold and special being a single, lesbian mom.

About a week before Kate and I broke up, I got the idea to have a baby as a performance piece. I'd charge hundreds of dollars a ticket and donate the money to a children's charity. Instead of tickets, everyone would get a beeper. When I went into labor, the beepers would go off and people would come to the theater.

The stage would be my birthing room. There'd be a birthing tub and a bed. My mom, Stephanie, Kate, and my midwife would be onstage with me. Each of us would make a speech to the audience about how we were feeling, who we were to each other, what we wanted for the baby. Nothing would be scripted. The show would be heartfelt and real and full of suspense. The more I talked about it to Kate, the more excited I got about the idea.

Kate got scared.

The reality of giving birth is deadly serious and scary and more exhausting than anything I've ever experienced. Childbirth is much more than an exercise like Outward Bound. It is not a performance.

During that last hour of labor, when I was stripped bare in every way, I asked my mom and Stephanie to leave. I couldn't smile for the camera. I couldn't even complain.

Nothing, until a baby tore though my vagina, had shown me my limits and taught me to accept what is.

I was flat on my back, ripped and worn and bleeding. My

baby lay on top of me for a few minutes before I lifted her up to see that she was a girl. I held her and marveled at her and cried while she cried and felt the most intense love and closeness I have ever known. Birth was ours, my baby's and mine.

My mom and Stephanie came in, and Tashi lifted her head, looking for my breast. Dana took my boob like it was a cow's teat and directed it into Tashi's mouth. Dana had had her fingers inside me for hours, guiding my baby through my vagina, but right then I felt uncomfortable with the way she handled me without asking.

I said: "Excuse me, Dana, that's my tit."

## Acknowledgments

One of the most fun and satisfying parts about writing a book, for me, is getting to thank the people who helped me. These are the same people who always help me, with everything. I can't possibly thank them enough, but I will try.

Thank you to the friends who believe in me even when I don't: Ida Dupont, Beth Reinhard, Karyn Nierenberg Tessler, and Andrea Stern. Also Lauren, who continues to show me how to love. And Stephanie Howard. No one has helped me more with this book or with this life.

Thanks to my mom, Bonnie Dubbin Askowitz, who taught me everything and taught me well.

Thanks to my readers: Elaine Bleiberg, Karin Cook, Jeff Cellers, John Faust, Ann Harrington, Yashar Hedayat, Nicky Herriot, Michael Jago, Ellen Kaplan, Steven Kaplan, Goldie Kossow, Elizabeth Marsh, Rod Menzies, Margaret Owens, Julie Saltman, Elijah Selby, Bob Spitz, Kerry Stone, Elizabeth Ussery. And Heather Maidat, my most attentive reader. And Patricia Owens for so many readings and love.

Thanks to my LA writing group and Terrie Silverman with CreativeRites. Everyone should take her class. Thanks to my Miami writing group and Dennis Ross for taking the writing personally.

I am so thankful for Stephanie Abou, my agent. She is classy. She is so much more than an agent to me, but I love that she's my agent. And Felice Newman and Frédérique Delacoste, my editors. They are classy too. Also Mark Rhynsburger, for making the copy pretty.

Thanks to my brother, Tony, for always supporting me and showing no signs of jealousy, even when I could beat him in tennis, which I acknowledge was a long time ago. And Lisa for being such a good sport and for being my friend. And Sue Fox, who will always be my family. Thanks to Bob, who doesn't worry too much about incriminating himself in front of me. And Elsa, for understanding me when I was a bitch. Thanks to my dad, who has given me so much. He read this book and still said I was his hero. He is mine too. And thanks to Danielle, Natalie, and Rachel, my original inspirations.

In some ways, a nanny is more important than a partner. Thank you to Reyhan Vural and family: Buse, Alper, and Eddie. Wendy Kirby and family: George, Victoria, Jessica,